# FROM THE COTTON FIELD TO THE WHITE HOUSE

AUTOBIOGRAPHY MOTIVATION

*My Incredible Journey*
"A BOOK EVERYONE SHOULD READ"

## MARTHA DIXON

FOREWORD BY RODNEY E. SLATER
FORMER U.S. SECRETARY OF TRANSPORTATION

Copyright © 2023 Martha Dixon.

All rights reserved. No part of this book may be reproduced, stored, or transmitted by any means—whether auditory, graphic, mechanical, or electronic—without written permission of both publisher and author, except in the case of brief excerpts used in critical articles and reviews. Unauthorized reproduction of any part of this work is illegal and is punishable by law.

ISBN: 979-8-88640-463-0 (sc)
ISBN: 979-8-88640-464-7 (hc)
ISBN: 979-8-88640-465-4 (e)

Because of the dynamic nature of the Internet, any web addresses or links contained in this book may have changed since publication and may no longer be valid. The views expressed in this work are solely those of the author and do not necessarily reflect the views of the publisher, and the publisher hereby disclaims any responsibility for them.

One Galleria Blvd., Suite 1900, Metairie, LA 70001
1-888-421-2397

In memory of my father James G. Smith,
my mother Beatrice Cook Smith,
and my twin Mary Smith.

With love and admiration
my husband Huie L. Dixon,
and my Son Christopher L. Dixon.

Special thanks to cover designer Denise Borel Billups.

Edited by Jerry Payne.

Thanks to Hughes & Hughes, Attorneys-at-law.

Special thanks to Hillary Rodham Clinton.

# CONTENTS

Foreword ................................................................................ vii

Introduction ........................................................................... ix

Prologue ................................................................................. xv

Chapter 1    A White House Guest ................................... xv

Chapter 2    James Garfield Smith ................................... xix

Chapter 3    Mother's Story ................................................ 2

Chapter 4    A Family of Twenty-Two ............................... 5

Chapter 5    Family Protector – Family Fear ..................... 11

Chapter 6    Legacies ......................................................... 19

Chapter 7    Siblings ......................................................... 26

Chapter 8    School Days .................................................. 56

Chapter 9    Making My Own Way .................................. 83

Chapter 10  A Family of My Own .................................... 90

Chapter 11  Discovered by the Clintons ........................... 95

Chapter 12  Businesswoman ............................................. 102

Chapter 13  Dixon Manufacturing ................................... 105

Chapter 14  Dr. Moor ....................................................... 114

Chapter 15  Politics .......................................................... 119

Chapter 16  Regrouping .................................................... 135

Chapter 17  Friends and Reflections ................................. 139

Appendix: Correspondences, Notes & Newspaper Clippings ........ 147

# FOREWORD

One of twenty siblings born and reared in rural Arkansas, near a place called Hope, Martha Dixon overcame early hardship to become an accomplished businesswoman and state political party leader, a friend of a future President, William Jefferson Clinton, and his wife, current U.S. Secretary of State Hillary Rodham Clinton. This is her story.

It is a revealing, thought-provoking one that not only tells about Martha, but also about her remarkable hardworking and religious family. Her early life centered on her brothers and sisters, including four sets of twins; her father, James Garfield Smith, from McNeal, Arkansas; and her mother, Beatrice Cook (Smith). A preacher, farmer, and land owner, James Smith donned pinstriped shirts for his Sunday work, replacing the crisply starched khaki shirts and pants he wore daily. He was a disciplinarian, who cherished the soil, protected his family, and believed earnestly in the power of prayer.

Like her father, Martha's mother, born in Okolona, Arkansas, was also a role model. Beatrice Cook and her siblings worked as sharecroppers growing up. Beatrice lost her mother in the child-birth of a sibling, the loss affecting Beatrice greatly, making her particularly sensitive to the love and care of her children and a host of grandchildren, nieces, and nephews who, seeking refuge, were raised in her household as her own children. Martha describes her mother as the "rock" of the family and the thread that held the family together during tough times.

With her skill as a seamstress, Martha uses the imagery and techniques of her chosen craft to ground her story in the rich history of her parents and grandparents, the backdrop providing the straight grain line – the line imprinted on the pattern of one's life – before the binding of the complex and varying fabrics into items worthy of admiration, capable of use, and deserving of praise. Martha pointedly, persuasively, and palpably argues that our indi-vidual lives require the same kind of care, stitching, and attention to detail to make for a purposeful life that "holds and hangs well."

A clear-eyed reading of Martha's story will surely provide you with a blueprint for living, creating in her words, "...a rich, empowering and fulfilling existence that will have form and function [and] will hang right."

I am proud to call Martha Dixon a friend, and I know you will be moved, profoundly touched, and inspired by her life story.

**–Rodney E. Slater**
Former U.S. Secretary of Transportation

# INTRODUCTION

I sat down to write this book over ten years ago but never found the time until now to finish it. It is just as well. Much has happened in the past ten years, and much has been learned. Life is like that – a constant source of education. One never stops learning, at least so long as one is paying attention to what the world has to teach. For me, the world has taught me much. It continues to do so.

This is an inspirational book about struggles, survival, and motivation. I started out with nothing, and yet eventually went on to run a very successful, very profitable company. I count among my many customers Tyson Foods, one of the largest meat producers in the world, and Wal-Mart, one of the largest companies in the world period. Individuals I have worked with include Presidential First Lady Hillary Clinton, an important customer, and a very good friend.

I have seen great struggles and poverty, and yet I have over-come them. Dixon Manufacturing – my company – could only have seemed like a pipe dream to anyone who knows of where I began in life. My whole career, and the many connections I have made, would seem the stuff of fairy tales to the little, bashful girl that I once was, picking cotton in the hot Arkansas sun. And yet, the dream became real. I'd like to share with you how that came to be.

More than just about me, this book is also about the struggles of my family. I was one of twenty children, born and raised in poverty. The unending challenges that we faced as a family forged a bond between my siblings and me, a bond that transformed a childhood from nothing more than a daily fight for survival into a special time that would strengthen and motivate me for the rest of my life. It is my hope that the reader will find inspiration in my family's stories of struggle and survival.

Perhaps, in your life, you have found yourself in the proverbial tunnel and have stopped dead in your tracks, believing that there is no light at the end. I can tell you that I have been through the tunnel, and there *is* a light at the end. But it is at the darkest points of the tunnel where we find out what we're truly made of. It is at these moments where we are called upon to be our strongest and to rely the most on our faith – faith that the universe has a plan for each of us, faith that if we just keep moving forward, one slow step at a time, we will ultimately get to where we are meant to be. We will emerge from the tunnel.

I set out a decade ago to write a book for those stumbling through life, finding themselves believing that there is no hope for tomorrow. If this sometimes sounds like you, I encourage you to read on. My hope is that if you are at a point in life where you're doing little but crawling through it, the stories gathered here will make you want to walk. If you are walking, they will make you want to run. If you are running, they will make you want to fly. Most importantly, I hope that you will be absolutely convinced that your potential is immeasurable, and your success is limited only by your imagination, dedication, and investment in yourself.

All my life I have measured and stitched fabric of any and all kinds to create a variety of garments. Like garment making, sometimes in life your stitches may veer to the right and sometimes they might veer to the left. But you can use your tape measure to get back on track, just as I have throughout my life – one stitch at a time. I have always tried to make sure the pattern of my life is a good one, so that others can follow my blueprint as they endeavor upon their own journeys. What I've learned is that, when you make a dress or a gown, if you do a good job, your customers will come back. If you measure and stitch your pattern of life well, then others will follow.

I have always worked from a pattern, either one that I created or one that was created by someone else, as when I was a student, for example, or was just learning to sew. Patterns are like a design or a road map for a garment. They help guide the seamstress. Life, even with its unpredictable ups and downs, can benefit from a well-developed pattern or roadmap. With the right tools you can make sure you are prepared for any challenges that come your way.

First and foremost, you must be ever aware of your straight "grain" line, the line that is imprinted on the pattern of your own life, your blueprint for creating a rich, empowering, and fulfilling existence that will have form and function, will "hang right", and will show the world the best of you. It is when we get off our grain line that we are the most in danger of losing our way, of getting away from the person we are meant to be, of coming up short of having the life we can have – the life we dreamt about as children, the life that can become ours if we have the courage to follow it, and the self-discipline and awareness to stick to the path.

Maybe this book can be a guide for you, for I have always stuck to my pattern to ensure that I would meet my goals. Know that as you read this, attaining your goals is possible, too. I hope you find your own way through life. I hope you know where your grain line runs. And I hope you have the faith to know that, just like me, you too can overcome whatever obstacles are thrown in your way.

Recognized as one of the "Top 100 Women of Arkansas" by Arkandad Business Magazine, and the recipienct of the numerous awards for her entrepreneurship, political work, and community service, Martha Dixon rose from abject poverty to the height of her profession. Founder of Dixon Manufacturing, as well as other successful enterprises, Ms. Dixon's meteoric career took her all the way from the cotton fields of Arkansas to the Lincoln Bedroom of the White House and beyond. Dress designer for First Lady Hillary Clinton (her presidential Gala gown remains on display at the Truman Library. Ms. Dixon's stellar reputation and the entrepreneurial spirit combined for one of the great success stories of our time.

*Martha sitting on the Lincoln Bed, the White House.*

PROLOGUE

# A WHITE HOUSE GUEST

"Sit on top of it and we'll take a photo," insisted Carolyn.

"Oh, my. I dare not," I replied, still wide-eyed.

"C'mon, Mom, after all, you're going to be sleeping on it tonight!" said Chris. I guessed he was right about that, so I climbed up on Mr. Lincoln's bed while Carolyn, member of Hillary Clinton's staff, took a photo. Surely, I thought, this had to be a dream.

Earlier that day, Chris and I had been whisked from the Washington airport to the White House in a long, shiny limo. Once inside the White House, as guests of the Clintons, we were allowed access to pretty much everywhere. We had walked around the grounds, ambled through the Rose Garden, lingered on the South Portico, watched the kitchen staff preparing that day's menu, strolled down the corridors, through the Roosevelt Room, the State Dining Room, even the Oval Office. Chris had come upon Socks, the famous First Cat and the two had spent a very good portion of the morning playing together.

And now here I was in the room I'd be sleeping in tonight – the famed Lincoln Bedroom. It was beautiful. I had been told something of the history; the room was originally used as an office by Lincoln. During the Truman administration it was rebuilt and dedicated to him, made into a bedroom making use of several pieces of furniture that were used by Lincoln and even by previous administrations. The bed itself, the bed I was sitting on having my picture taken, was a beautiful rosewood design with a huge headboard behind me that had been purchased by Mary Todd Lincoln herself. Displayed on a nearby desk was an original copy of the Gettysburg Address, written in Abe's own handwriting. I thought of the many people who had stayed in that room through the years, the Presidents and dignitaries, the rich and powerful and famous – the people who had slept in that very bed.

Later that night, I lay awake on that bed and I reflected on the events that had led me there. I thought about my relationship with the Clintons through the years – my designs for Hillary's gown for Bill's Governor Inauguration in Arkansas, and years later the gown for the Presidential Gala. I thought about the time years before when, poor and struggling, I had walked into dress shops all around Little Rock with my dresses, just hoping that somebody would give me and my fledgling business a chance, and how one shop finally did, and how Ann McCoy, administrator of the Governor's Mansion, happened to walk into that shop one day, see one of my silk creations and know immediately that it would appeal to Hillary.

I thought of my mother, too. And I began to cry. It seemed impossible that I could be here. Mama wouldn't have believed it, either – her daughter, one of twenty children, raised in an old wooden house the children's father, a poor sharecropper, had built by his own hand. The long, hot, Arkansas days picking cotton and peas; long, cold nights spent on a mattress stuffed with dry grass from the field. Her daughter, with nothing to look forward to but a back-breaking life of the same poverty she herself had known. Her daughter, who had started out with nothing but a talent for sewing, was now a guest at the White House. My business had grown from those weary days when I'd been pounding the pavement in Little Rock, and now I was the owner of a successful company. There would be more to come, as well. But on that night, lying wide awake in the Lincoln Bedroom, reflecting on my life, it seemed nothing less than miraculous that I had come this far.

And I couldn't help but think about where I'd been.

# CHAPTER ONE

# JAMES GARFIELD SMITH

When we think of family, usually things like foundation and bonding come to mind. Extended families and generations are produced with the coming together and binding of two or more families, families which are grounded in their own foundations, with their own complexities and various dynamics.

Often, the seamstress or tailor must bind together complex and varying fabrics, like heavy hems and appliqués. Then he or she may use something called bonding web, a light, mesh-like material used to stick layers of fabric together. Thinking about the stories of my father's and mother's families, I realize some relatives seem to have had the effect of a bonding web, most especially my mother, who did her best to keep our family together.

But it is with my father that my story truly begins.

James Garfield Smith was the grandson of slaves. From McNeil, Arkansas, his mother's family, the Parhams, owned a great deal of land. Many of the Parham family members could pass for white even though they were of African-American descent.

As we heard it, James's great grandparents on the Parham side were from Georgia and his great-grandmother was raped by her white master there. James's grandfather, Ebenezer Parham, married Josephine and, sometime after the Emancipation, moved to McNeil, a small rural town of about 3,000 in southern Arkansas that consisted of little more than some wooded land with a railroad running through it.

Josephine and Ebenezer had eighteen children. James's mother, Roxie Ann, was the eighth child born to them. She lived in McNeil where she later met and married Samuel Smith.

My father had two sisters, Lula and Josephine; and two brothers, Robert and William. Robert had two children, Robert, Jr., who everybody just called Bob, and a daughter named Rachel. I never knew very much about Rachel, and I saw Bob about five times in my life. He lived in Okolona, Arkansas, a small town of about 1,500 people, twenty-five miles from Arkadelphia, the closest town to the rural area from which I am from. Both he and Uncle William passed away when I was very young. I do know that Bob was about fifty-six when he died, leaving six children – three girls and three boys. I sometimes bump into one of them when I'm in town shopping.

My father's sister, Lula, the oldest of the girls, was very self-centered and considered herself to be very pretty because of her fair complexion. She thought it somehow made her better than the other siblings. Josephine, on the other hand, had a light brown complexion yet was a much more loving person. Josephine left Arkansas and lived in Ohio where she worked as a nurse. She didn't want to leave, but it was the 1930s, and at that time blacks had greater opportunities for better jobs in the northern cities. It was not at all uncommon for young black men and women to leave their families in the rural south for northern cities like New York, Chicago, or Cleveland, creating something of an exodus in the south for blacks.

Josephine's husband lived in Arkansas and she came home twice a year to visit. This arrangement seemed to work well for them. But she and James and the other siblings never visited their parents, nor did they visit each other. They worked constantly, never finding the time to visit each other, and never having the desire to visit their mother or father, both of whom had been very cruel to them. James and his brothers were beaten often by his parents, and at the tender age of eleven, James made the decision to run away. Lula and Josephine were spared the beatings, but all the children ultimately felt compelled to leave their abusive home and marry at early ages.

Ironically, after my grandfather died, Roxie Ann, my grandmother – no longer able to live by herself – would come to live with us. After all those years, Roxie Ann still had cruelness in her. I was about twelve-years-old and I remember it well. I never encountered her cruelness with her walking stick, maybe because I was old enough to get out of the way, but my younger sister Ruth did. My grandmother hit her with that stick many times.

She did many other cruel things to us as well. One day she urinated in a cup and tried to make my brother Henry drink it. When he wouldn't, she told my father that we would not drink the "tea" that she had made. She told father a lot of lies about us kids, lies that he always believed, even though he had lived his first eleven years with her and knew firsthand her cruel ways. And no matter how much we protested our innocence, her lies always resulted in whippings by Father.

I didn't see it at the time, but years later I would come to understand my father better by considering his mother. As much as we try, we can't always escape the environment we come from. I don't pretend to understand the demons that must have been raging within the mind of my grandmother – to me she was just cruel – but there's no doubt the effect they had on my father. Father was a stern man – harsh and very often cruel himself. I didn't see the connection as a child. As a child I loved the man and respected him. He was my father, after all. But there were many times I was afraid of him. And there were many times I hated him.

James got his first job when he was fourteen years old, working on a farm for a white family. He performed mostly manual labor, picking cotton and vegetables, pulling hay, milking cows, and feeding the hogs.

For awhile, he drifted from farm to farm, working for food and shelter. The farmers gave James food from their families' leftovers. Sometimes the food would be nothing more than bread and water. James would also go into the woods and hunt for nuts and berries. The families he worked for would allow him to sleep in their barns, on the hay, with the livestock.

As James got older and began demanding to be paid fair wages, the farmers balked. One night some friends of a white plantation owner in Mississippi grabbed him and took him to the Mississippi plantation where he was forced into work as a slave. Though there were other young men on the plantation who were also slaves, James was the youngest. One side of the plantation bordered the Mississippi River, the other was guarded by watch dogs. The men were worked all day and locked up at night. James had managed to escape the beatings from his parent in McNeil, but was now subject to beatings at the hands of the proprietors of a plantation that was straight out of pre-Civil war days.

James worked on the plantation for five years, eventually coming up with a plan to escape. He cut down a tree and let it lie for close to a year to make sure it was fully dried out. Then one evening before the plantation owner could lock him up, he placed the tree in the Mississippi River, climbed on top, and floated down the river to freedom. Far enough downstream, he knew he'd be safe from the dogs. He floated down the tumultuous river undetected by man and beast for a full day, ultimately landing on the opposite shore to begin an arduous trek back towards home. Years later, whenever he would retell the story to us, he would always say that, "God was with me." And considering the dangers, I'd have to agree; it truly was a miracle that my father survived.

But Arkansas wasn't home to James any more than any other state really was in those days of his youth, and so he drifted, all around the south looking for work. This was unfortunately all too common for young black men at the time, even continuing on with my own brothers.

Around 1919 James finally settled in Oklahoma where he had family of a sort. His sister Lula had married a man named Bus Cook, who happened to have had two daughters, Lucile and Beatrice, both of whom had moved to Oklahoma. The latter of the two would eventually become my mother.

# CHAPTER TWO

# MOTHER'S STORY

Beatrice Cook Smith was born in Okolona, Arkansas. Her mother, Carrie Cook, died when Beatrice was just four years old in a way that was all too common in those days – she died while giving birth.

My mother had one sister, Lucile, and two brothers, Forrest and George, with George being the youngest. Her father, Bus Cook, did the best he could raising the children after their mother passed away, working as a sharecropper. It was far from easy. One day he almost lost all of the children to a horrific fire. Working in the field, he looked up to see their house suddenly engulfed in flames. He ran into the burning structure, saving all of the kids in time. But it came at a cost. Bus had inhaled a lot of smoke in the process and he soon developed asthma. Though a picture of health before the fire, he hardly had a day without coughing or difficulty breathing afterwards. Bus was never the same, hardly able to work from then on. He died from a stroke at the age of seventy-three.

My mother and her siblings worked in the fields with their father. Times were hard and Mother recalled suffering through a number of winters with no shoes to protect her feet. One freezing day, her feet felt so cold she thought she would urinate on them to keep them warm.

And for a while it helped. But after a few minutes her feet were colder than ever. Though she would face the hardship of cold feet many more times, she never tried that particularly solution again.

Although being raised without a mother was hard, my mother and her siblings came to discover that being raised by a stepmother who cared nothing for you could be harder. Bus Cook had eventually married James Smith's oldest sister, my Aunt Lula. The children thought their lives would be better with a woman in the house, not to mention the three new children that Lula brought with her. It meant more playmates, and more people with whom to share the work. But it turned out their lives didn't become better at all.

Lula's complexion was very light and my mother and her siblings were dark-complexioned. The children's new stepmother mistreated them because of this. She always made them enter the house through the back door. When she fed them, she set their plates on the floor where they would have to eat. Her own children, meanwhile, she adored. And when Lula and Bus eventually had two children of their own – two boys named Claude and Hop – they, too, were adored by Lula.

Beatrice and her sister Lucile were close growing up and as they grew older they became even closer. Having lost their mother, the two sisters had come to depend upon each other for support. When they were old enough, they left their father and stepmother's home. The year was 1925. Beatrice was fifteen and Lucile was seventeen. They moved to Oklahoma where together they were able to scratch out enough of a living for rent and food. About a year later, their step uncle, James Smith, still drifting around from state to state, came to town and moved in with them.

James was a very good looking man and the story was that he played around with both sisters. My mother fell in love with him and they married. Soon, they began having children. When they first married my mother weighed ninety-eight pounds and wore a size six-and-a-half shoe. Beatrice Smith, the mother that I knew, weighed three-hundred pounds and wore a size ten. She had put on weight with each pregnancy following the birth of her first child and was never able to lose it. But she was a strong woman and al-ways carried her weight well. She could do far more work than the average woman. Even in her later years, she would chop her own wood to put in her old wood stove to keep warm. And she would often be out in her garden, plowing the earth with a walking tiller.

Mother was the rock of my family. She was my rock. She had enough love to dole out to her twenty children, and all of her grandchildren and great grandchildren, treating us all the same. Though there was real love between her and my father, the two were very different people. The way they raised us, what we were able to learn from each, the challenges we faced in our daily struggle for survival – it all made for an interesting childhood.

## CHAPTER THREE

# A FAMILY OF TWENTY-TWO

In a few short years, James and Beatrice were raising two girls, Annie Mae and Eula Mae, and two boys, Samuel and James, Jr. They moved back to Arkansas where they worked as sharecroppers, growing a variety of vegetables – sweet potatoes, beans, peas, greens, tomatoes, okra, and squash. They shared what they grew with the owner of the land, sometimes for money, sometimes for food. It was a daily struggle and never so bad as when the cold winters set in. During those hard months, the four children would have to do as Father had done, often going into the woods in search of nuts and berries to eat. When the owner of the land died, it came to light that he had failed to pay his property taxes. The land reverted to the state and Mother and Father saw their chance to buy some of the land they had toiled upon. For a small amount of money, they were able to secure forty acres of it. At thirty-nine and thirty-four years of age, respectively, my father and mother were now home-owners, in full charge of a substantial amount of land.

*The family home that Father had built.*

James used the timber from the land to build a nine-room house with an outside toilet. The house came complete with a living room, dining room, and kitchen, in addition to six bedrooms.

James and Beatrice continued having children, sixteen more, half of which were four sets of twins. Mother would frequently tell the story of having one child on one breast and another child on the other. The first set, Amos and Andy (Andrew), were born in 1930. The second set, Paul and Silas, were born in 1935 in Paducah, Texas, on one of our parents' cotton-picking excursions. The third and final set of boy twins, Jacob and Joseph, were born in 1939. And the final set of twins, my sister Mary and I, were born in the winter of 1946.

In between were Abraham, Isaac, Josephine, Henry, Aaron, Moses, Mark, and Ruth. For sleeping arrangements, Mother and Father had their own room, of course, with a large iron bed. The children shared the remaining five bedrooms, with three iron beds in each. The older children slept in those while the younger children were relegated to sleeping on the floor.

Sometimes the children would have to vacate a bedroom so that a stranger could make use of it. As far back as I can remember, it seemed we always had strangers coming in and out. Sometimes the stranger would be a woman, sometimes a man. In his travels, my father would often pick up hobos and weary travelers in need of shelter and a meal, and bring them home. Father always said he couldn't stand the thought of seeing people in need and not helping them. He had been in those traveler's shoes much in his life. His generosity in this regard was just one example of the many complexities that were inherent in him. On the one hand, he could be viciously cruel to his own children, yet on the other hand, he could be full of compassion for a complete and total stranger.

In addition to the house itself, my father built all the furniture therein. In particular I remember the dining room table. It had a beautiful shine and was complete with matching chairs. But even at a full six feet by eight, it wasn't quite large enough to accommodate everybody. Father would always sit at the head of the table, Mother sometimes sitting next to him. But most of the times, Mother would either eat before or after everybody else so that the children could sit around the table together with Father. Often the children would do this in shifts, with the older siblings eating first and then the younger ones, although sometimes Mother would prepare a special place on the floor for the youngest of the children.

Mother cooked most the meals but sometimes she would work on the farm with the rest of us, in which case she would leave Josephine, one of the older sisters, to do the cooking. Meals usually consisted of whatever we raised on the farm and in our garden. At times we had enough to eat and at other times we didn't. Our favorite meals were on Sundays, because on Sundays we always had some type of meat, typically chicken, raised right on our farm. Side dishes might be beans and greens from the garden. Once we were all settled around the table, one of the siblings would lead the family in reciting the Lord's Prayer. Every-body would eventually have their turn at leading the meal prayer.

Father wasn't fond of any kind of playing around the table. One day when we were about to eat, my young brother Aaron and my niece Evelyn were playing. Father told them firmly to stop. When they didn't, he picked up a glass and threw it, hitting Aaron in the face with it, producing a gash that required ten stitches. It took Aaron many years to forgive Father. Through the years there were many things that my siblings and I have forgiven our father for. But there are other things we will never forget.

Nobody was spared the manual labor that the farm required and it seemed as though all of the work was back-breaking work. And we worked for other farmers, too. Most of them white. From sun up till sundown, we'd pick and chop cotton. We'd barter our labor for food, picking peas "on the half," as it was called, with the landowner taking half of every bushel of peas we picked and letting us keep the other half. We used this barter system for other vegetables, too – beans, corn, sweet potatoes, and tomatoes. We worked like this until I was in the eleventh grade. I hardly remember having time to play, or make friends with other children. Whatever time we did find to play, my brothers, sisters, and – later – my nieces and nephews, would play with each other – marbles, maybe, or ring around the rosy and hopscotch.

Although the best part of the day should have been sundown, finally getting a reprieve from the hard work in the fields, the only respite was fitful and comfortless rest upon iron-framed beds topped with mattresses filled with whatever soft material was available. Usually it was hay from the barn or even grass from the fields in which we worked. Neither was very comfortable for an aching body, but I preferred the give of the fine blades of dry grass to the unyielding stiffness of the hay. I remember spending many a day pulling grass from our field and stuffing it into an opening on the side of my mattress.

As tough as times were, Father always managed to find enough work for us to survive. My father was an entrepreneur before people knew what the word meant. He had a wide variety of skills and was knowledgeable about many different things. Though primarily a farmer, at one time he owned a grocery store. He sold vegetables from our garden out of that store, along with homemade medicines. He even sold spring water by the dipper from our well. He'd also sell vegetables up and down the street, peddling them from house to house. In my lifetime I never knew my father to work for anybody but himself. He always taught his children that it was best to own your own business. It was a lesson I never forgot, and one that would profoundly influence my life.

Father was a smart man, almost completely self-educated. He bought all kinds of books and read all the time. Whenever he would come across a book, he'd read it, and whenever he wanted to know about something, he'd study about it diligently. He could talk on a variety of subjects and people often mistook him for a college graduate. In truth, his formal education didn't reach beyond the sixth grade.

Father was an excellent Bible scholar, too, and I can still see his big family Bible resting on the coffee table where he kept it, so large that it almost covered the whole table. We called it simply "The Book" and my father cherished it. It was what he used to teach from and what he lived by. It was his love of that book that led him to give most of his children biblical names. Of course one of his most beloved passages from the Bible was the Proverb about sparing the rod and spoiling the child. We learned that one first-hand on many occasions. I have "The Book" in my home now, where, though torn and ragged, it remains a prized possession.

As voracious a reader as my father was, he never took the time to teach his children. His books were sacred to him. They were his and his alone. He'd keep them in his room, not allowing us to touch them. We would have no access to books until we started school.

Even if it had been important to Father to make sure his children developed reading and writing skills, it seemed to us as though he never stood still long enough to do so. He was always busy at his store or gone on trips to sell his fruits and vegetables. For us, work took center stage in each of our lives practically from our very first steps. We were often kept out of school to work in the fields and had to fight for whatever education we could get on our own.

Two Sundays out of each month Father would preach in our home to his family. The other two Sundays he would preach in local churches, donning his pinstriped suit. He was always well-dressed, even during the week. Mother would always starch and iron his khaki shirts and pants, which he loved and would wear complete with necktie. A lot of men who farmed like Father only dressed up when they planned a visit to town, but Father preferred his crisp khaki shirt, necktie, and slacks whether he spent the day in town, or out in the field.

Always well-groomed and at nearly six feet tall, father was a man who drew quite a bit of attention. Even as a child I noticed that most women took a second look at Father. I never saw him with another woman but it was known that he had many other women. He and Mother separated several times, but being the kind of person she was, Mother always took him back.

Notwithstanding his faults, Father was a role model for us children. We all learned a lot about work and self discipline from him. If nothing else, he was a hard worker, and knew how to survive, values he passed on to us. I don't think it's coincidence that, today, many of us are hard working entrepreneurs who own our own businesses.

# CHAPTER FOUR

# FAMILY PROTECTOR – FAMILY FEAR

The forty acres that my father purchased and built our home upon were incorporated in South Central, Arkansas, which is a community about six miles outside of Arkadelphia. The population of our little community was probably never more than 150 at any one time, a tiny number compared with the roughly 11,000 residents of the more densely populated nearby Arkadelphia.

Father's acreage was surrounded by white farmers. Many of them resented the fact that blacks now owned land adjacent to theirs. It was often necessary for Father to be prepared to defend himself, his land, and his family, and so he always carried a gun. The whites showed their hostility in numerous ways. We had neighbors who would move the fence my father had erected around our property while making it seem as though they were innocently fixing their own fence. Little by little they would slowly move our fence backwards from their property. This went on for several months until Father had

*Father's original fence*

decided he'd had enough. When he noticed his neighbor once again "mending" his fence, he sat down on his side of the property line with a gun by his side, keeping a watchful eye on the repair process and staying out there all day until the job was done. From then on, our fence re-mained in its proper place.

Father often patrolled his land on foot, but eventually he was able to afford a used tractor which he would drive around the farm whenever he would get the chance. In addition to protecting the land from neighbors, he was diligent about protecting it from the elements as well. He built terraces all over the acreage so that the water would run off and go in different directions, preventing the soil from being washed away.

Putting on his carefully starched and crisply ironed khakis and suspenders, Father would ride over the forty acres inspecting the large garden to see how the crops were faring. Of course he would also check to see if we had done what he had told us to do, usually picking peas, okra, turnip, and mustard greens, butter beans, cucumber, squash, cantaloupe, watermelon, and all types of fruits – peaches, plums, pears, and so many others.

When there was enough fruits and vegetables to make a truckload, Father would have us load the pickup truck until it was full. Then he would take off for several days, slowly driving his truck through town and beyond. People came to expect him and would run out to the road to greet him and buy his fresh produce. He became well known for his herbal medicines, too, and he would sell those out of the truck along with the fruits and vegetables. The medicines were so popular that after his death many of his customers would ask my mother if she'd kept the formulas. Unfortunately, she had not, and although we children had dug all the roots father used to make his herbal remedies, we didn't know which roots went into which medicines, nor the combinations of them. After several days on the road, Father would come back with his truck empty, and the process would begin anew.

His strictness notwithstanding, everyone has their favorite memories of Father and mine is riding along with him one day when he went to sell our fruits and vegetables. I sat in the worn seat next to him in the cab of the truck as he plowed down the road. He made up a song by naming all of the vegetables that were piled up in the back. I can still hear his booming voice: *Watermelon-cucumber-squash-cantaloupe-okra-beans-peas for sale!* I joined in and we sang that song over and over.

It's a memory that sits quite a bit at odds with other, less happy, memories. The cycle of abuse that began with my father's parents continued with Father. We children all loved him, in our own ways. But we all hated him, too, and in secret referred to him dishonorably as "Old Man." One of the most vicious incidents of his cruelty and abusiveness involved the very vegetables that we loaded into that pickup truck of his. One evening after dinner, my nine-year-old brother Henry and my eight-year-old nephew Edward were tasked with loading up the truck with watermelons so that Father could get an early start the next morning. Father was rightly proud of our watermelons; we raised some of the biggest and best ones in the county. But that night, when the household was asleep, Henry and Edward decided to pull two of the largest watermelons from the truck and eat them.

The next morning, when my father had discovered what the two boys had done, he was furious. He tied the hands of my brother and nephew to the back bumper of his truck, then began to beat them with a leather strap. Father beat them so severely that they begged the Lord for mercy, to which Father shouted, "Don't call on the Lord. Call on the devil! He is the one who told you to do what you have done!" Being children who just wanted the pain to stop, they promptly obeyed, proceeding to call on the devil. As a God-fearing, Christian child, it was chilling and heartbreaking for me to hear the boys pleading in that way. As hard as it might be to believe, when we get together today – the children of James Smith – we're actually able to laugh a little about such incidents.

For although my father's abusiveness may have driven a wedge between him and his children, it created a strong bond between all of us siblings and our nieces and nephews. We were afraid of him, but our love for each other made us very protective of each other. That was our best – perhaps only – protection against Father's volatile temper and irascible nature. It was not uncommon for one of us to sacrifice his or her own safety to protect that of another sibling, niece, or nephew.

My older brother Jacob did just that one time for me and my niece Evelyn. Father had ten cows and we children were to keep them in the pasture. He had just had the boys dust the greens with a pesticide to keep the insects from eating them. One cow got out of the pasture, ate some of the greens after they had been dusted, and died. Father was livid. He pulled the dead cow to the end of the acreage and took my two brothers Henry and Joseph along with him. He tied their hands to the dead cow's legs and left them there all night. It was mid-summer and it didn't take very long for the smell of the rotting carcass to attract vultures. My brothers were afraid and the rest of us kids were equally terrified for them. But Father had warned us if we cut them free or interfered in any way, we'd be sorry.

My niece and I couldn't stand to see Henry and Joseph suffering that way. We decided we were willing to take the beating and we cut them free the next day. When Father saw the boys had been cut loose, Jacob jumped in, taking both the blame and the resulting whipping.

Had my niece and I been found out, it would have been impossible to avoid the severe beating we would have been in line to receive for disobeying Father. Though the house was fairly large, there were few places to hide that Father didn't know about. Besides, it was far more dangerous to anger him further by challenging him, than to just take the beating and get it over with.

Henry learned this lesson the hard way. I can't even recall what minor thing he did to provoke Father's wrath one day, but when Father decided to punish him, Henry began running around the outside of the house. Father picked up a brick that was lying in the yard and threw it at him. My brother's small legs didn't allow him to outrun a large brick thrown with the force of a strong, angry, determined man. The brick struck Henry in the neck. The injury was temporary but I never remember seeing Henry run from Father again.

There was another incident involving Henry that stuck with me, too. After a series of bed-wetting episodes, Father decided to "cure" Henry's problem by tying a line around Henry's penis one night before he went to bed. The only effect it had was to provide Henry with a sore and swollen penis by the next morning. Father actually became concerned, thinking he might have done irreparable harm. He hadn't, but he never used that particular method again.

Around the house, we all had different jobs to do. One of my jobs was to pick the okra. I remember my father checking the okra patch and finding four hard pods of okra that I had left by accident. I fell to my knees and begged my father not to whip me, but it did no good. He got his fishing pole and beat me until the pole broke.

Neither begging nor having a good excuse protected me from a father who was eager to punish. Another one of my jobs was to dig up and store the Irish potatoes that Father grew. One day my mother asked me to bring some potatoes in and peel them for dinner. Naturally, I did what my mother asked me to do, but when my father came in and saw me peeling the potatoes, he got angry and beat me. It didn't matter to him that it hadn't been my intention to disobey him at all and that I was merely obeying the direction of Mother.

Whenever we would be sent out to pick berries for Father to sell, he would inspect our mouths afterwards, making us stick out our tongues. If he discovered we'd eaten any of the berries, we could be sure of getting smacked on the mouth. That was a punishment we could at least anticipate. My brothers had a little harder time calculating the risks when they were one day tasked with planting peas. They planted a few, but then decided it was too nice a day to spend planting the rest. They dug a whole and buried the bulk of the peas in it. The problem was, in just a few short weeks, new pea plants all came out of the ground in one particular spot. It wasn't too hard for Father to figure out what had happened, and the boys paid the price.

*Fred our mule look alike*

From milking the cows, to feeding the hogs and chickens, to plowing the fields, we all had our chores to do. Father couldn't afford a motorized plow, so we used mules for the job. All of our mules had been given names to suit their particular disposition. Now mules are generally stubborn and ornery animals, but Father had one he called Fred who seemed to be made of rocks he was so hard to persuade. Once when I had to plow the grounds with Fred, he gave me a terrible scare. We were going along just fine when Fred suddenly decided that he no longer wanted to cooperate. He re-fused to move from the spot he'd rested on and would no longer respond to any of my commands – giddyap (start, go faster), gee (turn right), or haw (turn left). Then he slowly ambled away and simply lay down on the ground. Unfortunately, where he decided to lay was in the middle of Father's prized watermelon patch.

Not wanting to risk ruining father's watermelons and getting the certain beating for it, I decided that my hide was worth more than Fred's. I took the ends of the reins and lashed him. When he finally got up, I was more than a little relieved to see that Father's precious watermelons were unharmed.

I wasn't always so lucky about escaping Father's ire. He was strict with all of us children and had unyielding rules which we dared not break. He ran the household in a regimented manner and there was little tolerance for things he believed were trivial and a waste of time. He didn't even allow his daughters to wear fingernail polish. We knew better than to try our father's patience by complaining about the rules or even asking him to consider changing his mind about them.

One summer day my older sister Eula, having moved out of the house by then, came home to visit. She brought home the most beautiful shade of fingernail polish. It was a bright, cheerful pink and it reminded me of posies. Even though I knew father would not allow me to wear it, I convinced Eula to give it to me and intended to keep it hidden in my bedroom until I had an opportunity to wear it away from the house.

For a few nights, every time I went to my room just before bed, I would steal a look at my posy pink nail polish by opening and closing the bottle. One night, I was no longer satisfied to just open the bottle and look at the polish. I had to see what it looked like on my nails. But I knew I couldn't risk having father see the polish on my fingernails, even if it was just painted on a single finger. Then I had an idea that, at the time, I believed to be very clever. I thought I would outsmart Father by painting my toe nails instead of my fingernails.

Sometime during the next day, my sister Josephine, who was older and more willing to challenge father, was popping her fingers. Of course this was a no-no in father's household because it was somehow associated with that other lascivious and forbidden activity – dancing. Father angrily yelled in from the other room demanding to know who was doing the finger popping. My sister, who had ignored my warnings to stop flirting with such danger, looked straight at me and my silent, unmoving fingers before yelling back out to Father that Martha was the culprit. My body shook when he ordered me into the room in the next instant because I knew what I was in for.

I understand now of course that it was just mischief on my sister's part but at the time I couldn't have hated her more. I knew I'd be unable to defend myself. Father could not be reasoned with once his anger was riled. And even if I would have been able to convince him of my innocence in the finger-popping scandal, there would be no hiding the fact that my toe nails were painted a bright posy pink. And because I was not wearing shoes, my contraband-covered toes would be in full view once I entered the room where father sat waiting to chide and possibly strike me.

I did, in fact, end up getting a terrible beating that day. As I look back on it, it was one of the few times I was actually due a justifiable whipping. After all, I had deliberately broken one of the rules of my father's house. What stung as badly as my whipping that day was the fact that I might have gotten away with it, had it not been for my sister Josephine.

If we faced anger from Father, we got nothing but kindness from our mother. It was an old-fashioned marital relationship with Father the clear master of the house. Mother always tried to be a good wife and a good mother. She was the thread that held the family together. When I was older, after Father died, my mother and I would sit up nights talking in her bed. We would talk about everything from her childhood to her relationship with my father. She used to tell me that he treated her so badly that she often preferred to see the back of his head than the front of his face – going, that is, rather than coming. No one in the house was safe from Father's anger and Mother was a target almost as frequently as we children were. Although she could be afraid of Father, she would often stand up for herself and her children. Though there were the constant rumors of the extra-marital relationships with other women, I think Father found mother too endearing to completely abandon her.

Mother and I had many candid conversations sitting up in her bed together and in one of those conversations, she told me something that would affect me my whole life. She said that father saw something in me that no one else saw. He told her that I was a survivor and that I would do well in life.

CHAPTER FIVE

# LEGACIES

Every September, after our fruits and vegetables had all been picked and sold, we would all load into the back of Father's truck, huddled underneath a tarp he had rigged to keep the wind and rain off of us, and we would migrate from our home to other parts of Arkansas and to parts of west Texas, Arizona, and Missouri where we would find work picking cotton. Sometimes other families from surrounding towns would tag along with us.

Mother came along and would sit in the front of the truck with Father. Usually, after finding work and spending a couple days with us, Father would then leave us and return home to take care of the homestead. It was left to Mother and the older siblings to keep us younger ones safe. Mother would send money back for Father to pay bills. One year she discovered that the bills had remained unpaid. It was said that Father had spent it on other women.

We were paid three cents per pound of cotton we picked. Sometimes our shoulders would get raw and sore from the backbreaking labor of picking cotton and the strain of pulling the heavy cotton sacks all day Monday through Friday and half the day on Saturday. The cotton sacks would be slung over our left shoulders all day long. Years and years of this burden took their toll. In time, my siblings and I began to notice that our left shoulders all sloped lower than our right ones. It happened to all of us, but it's more noticeable with the sisters. To this day, when one of us slips on a blouse or a t-shirt, the blouse or t-shirt slides downward on the left side. It's a constant reminder of where we've come from.

Saturday evening, we would go to town to get groceries and on Sunday we would wash our clothes. Sometimes the house that we would stay in would be in the middle of the cotton field, and would have holes in the roof and in the floor. Sometimes some of the windows would be broken and we would have to hang a cotton sack over them to keep out the rain and the dust. There was never any electricity in any of the houses we stayed in; light was provided by kerosene lanterns.

*Replica of the house we lived in while on cotton harvest.*

On the road, Mother worked hard to hold our large family together. When we returned, the money we had made would be used to pay the mortgage, but before winter was over we would have to get another mortgage in order to buy food. Each year my mother would buy a hundred pounds of meal and flour so we could eat through the winter months. By spring we would be out of food and we'd have to mortgage our land all over again.

We would come back from our picking trips in January to start school and of course we could never really catch up to the rest of the kids. It wasn't until I was in eleventh grade that I would spend more than half a year in school. We were the talk of the school among the teachers and the students. Most of the teachers never tried to help us learn, imaging us to be lost causes. Most of them looked through us as if we weren't there. Some of my siblings had no education, some first grade, some second, some beyond, into high school. Only two finished the twelfth grade. Even though my older sisters and brothers wanted to finish school it proved to be too hard for them to make it, especially with no support from either our parents or the school staff. One by one the older kids gave up.

One day Father got sick and didn't get better. For nearly a year he had seen one doctor after another, none of whom could tell him what was wrong. He could no longer work the land, could no longer ride his tractor over the forty acres, could no longer do what he loved to do. Occasionally I would see tears rolling down his face. He tried to hide it but couldn't and we would see him wiping his face every now and then.

Once, when Father asked me to trim his toe nails, I became agitated and started to cry because I knew that if I accidentally hurt him he'd probably still find the strength to give me a whipping, even as ill as he was becoming. One thing that will always linger in my mind is that fear so prevailed in my father's household that – even though he needed me and was vulnerable – I was too afraid to help him.

Confined to the house because of his illness, Father would sit in his old chair, getting weaker and weaker with each passing day. He worried about how Mother would survive after the illness took his life. After all of the running around, separation, and heartache my father caused my mother, she still loved him. Looking back, I think he still loved her, too.

Eventually, Father found out that he had leukemia. By the time he was properly diagnosed, it was too late. Knowing he was dying he told Mother that he did not want to die at home. He asked her if she'd take him to the hospital in Prescott, Arkansas. It was there that he died on September 16, 1960, within three days of his diagnosis. His last words to my mother were, "I only worry about you. Will the boys take care of you? If I knew that, I could die in peace."

Father taught us many things, but his legacy is unfortu-nately mired in a cycle of abuse, not to mention the lack of respect for his children's education. Just as God was with him on that day he floated to safety down the mighty Mississippi on a log, God must have been the guiding force behind my decision to take my father's books when he passed away. None of my other siblings wanted them anyway.

But I was not content to just take those books. I also wanted to take control of my education. I was the first of James Smith's children to attend college. I will always cherish the books and the accidental lesson father gave me to fight for my education. I promised myself that when I was old enough and had enough money I would buy all the books that my heart desired, and would read one after another. So far, I have done just that, having accumulated a plethora of books by various authors and placed them painstakingly in my library and all throughout my home. When I go to the bookstore I usually buy two or three books at a time – sometimes more. My husband Huie has amusedly asked me from time to time, "Aren't you going overboard with all of those books? Are you really going to read them all?" My answer to him is always yes.

Often I can see the influence Father had upon me. How does a poor girl from a tiny town in Arkansas make something of herself? It must start with resolve – the kind of gritty determination my father had always had. He never explicitly taught it to me; that wouldn't be his way. But I learned it from him just the same. I saw the way he refused to work in the employ of others, the way he always tried to do things right, to be the best he could be, the pride he took in his vegetables and in the farm. Father was many things, some not so good. But above all else, the man was determined. I often think about that determination, and at those moments, I can see the best of Father in me.

As for the worst of my father, his remaining children, to a one, have long since forgiven him. We all know that, in his way, the man loved us. He never said it, of course, but the evidence was there. Like on one hot summer day with me and my brother Moses.

*Replica of Father's old red tractor.*

We were riding along with Father on his tractor as he was cultivating the fields at the outer perimeter of the property. The tractor pulled the cultivator along with me sitting on one side of the tilling implement and Moses on the other. Our job was to add ballast and balance out the cultivator, but as kids we were just enjoying the ride. Then somehow Moses managed to get a foot caught in one of the blades. He howled in pain as the blade dug into his foot, severely cutting a toe. Father brought the tractor to an instant halt and in one fluid motion grabbed Moses, blood freely flowing from his bare foot, and spun out of the tractor seat, running with his son slung over his shoulder almost before he hit the ground. I ran behind, trying to keep up, but quickly lost ground to Father's huge strides. He carried Moses back to the house across forty acres that day. The look of concern I saw on his face is one I have always remembered. I knew at that moment how much the man loved each of us.

It was an easy thing to forget sometimes, with the whippings. But looking back, remembering the days when grandmother came to live with our family, we can all see the legacy that Father was unfortunately bequeathed. That he was not able to overcome it is pardonable, if not completely understandable. We, as his children, have broken the cycle, and in an ironic way, I'm sure he'd be proud of us for having done so – proud of the determination.

I've often thought he'd be proud of me and my accomplish-ments, too. He didn't live to see them, but if he had, I think he would have told me he was pleased. I like to think so anyway. He was, after all, a true entrepreneur. And he was one back in the days before most black men could even imagine themselves running successful businesses. I'd want to tell him I was proud of him for that, and grateful that he had, albeit unwittingly and unknowingly, passed that along to me. I'd want to tell him I love him, I'd want to embrace him. Although I must admit that even now I might still be afraid of my father, I'd like to think that he'd be gentle, that he'd embrace me back, knowing that a part of him – the better part – lives on in me.

After my father's death, we really got to know my mother. I remember the old wood stove on which she would do all her cooking. She sometimes would make as many as a hundred biscuits for breakfast. She was always singing or humming a song all day long. And she was always proud of her children. My mother lived for her children, and her children were her joy. In time, she lived for her grandchildren, too, all of them referring to her as "Big Mama".

Mother was a very strong, moral person who always tried to do the right thing. She made sure we were all were baptized at an early age. I know now the serious and sacred thing baptism is, but when I was baptized along with my brother and two nieces at the age of twelve, I really had no idea what it was all about. I did it only because my mother wanted me to. Needless to say I'm glad Mother had me baptized. And I wonder how many other children, or even adults, get baptized for no better reason than because someone else wants it. It seems we all do so many things to please others.

I never knew my mother to do anything wrong. My husband would say that he never met anyone who was as nice as my mother. And she was a strong woman, getting her strength, so far as I could tell, from an unending positive attitude. She always had something good to say about everyone. And when I would ask Mother why she was happy, she would just smile and say, "Life is just what you make out of it, and you can always find some good and some happiness if you look hard enough."

This, perhaps, is the biggest lesson I learned from my mother. A different lesson, of course, than what I learned from Father, but just as important in helping me become the person I am today. With her positive attitude, it was hard for her to remain down about things, no matter the difficulties she may have been having. Throughout my life, in my darkest moments, I have tried to remember to "look hard enough" for the happiness that is there. I often think that we spend too much time expecting happiness to just show up on our doorstep and loudly announce itself. It never does, of course. And yet it's there just the same. All we need do is know how to look. Mother taught me this. And I and my siblings hold onto the lesson to this day. With Mother, we all felt and had all the love anyone could ask for and more.

# CHAPTER SIX

# SIBLINGS

*A**ny seamstress aspiring to sewing or dressmaking greatness knows that before she begins her sewing project, she must make sure her fabric is straight. It is essential to getting the best finished garment. The methods for making sure of this vary depending on the fabric. As I prepared to write this chapter about my brothers and sisters, I thought about all the many different kinds of fabrics I have used over the years and how like those fabrics, we are all different. Yet most of us went through a time in our lives when somebody had to "straighten" us in an attempt to make sure there was a good end result.*

Though Mother and Father influenced me profoundly, so did my siblings and other relations, to varying degrees. Some I was closer to than others. Annie Mae, for example, whom we just called Mae, had left home before I was born. But I would spend time at her house, in nearby Arkadelphia, playing hop scotch, tic-tac-toe, and hide-and-seek with her oldest child, my niece Evelyn. Evelyn was a year and five months older than I, and my best friend growing up.

Mae would give birth to seven other children, two of whom died at birth. She was a lovely person, with a beautiful complexion, and brown, shoulder-length hair. I was always happy to visit her home and see Evelyn, and Evelyn was always happy to come visit me. Mae and her husband had a six-room house and all of her girls shared the same bedroom. If I would stay overnight, I would share a bed with Evelyn.

As teenagers, Evelyn and I would always double date. At least, that is, once I was old enough. My mother had a strict rule that we girls had to be sixteen before we could date. When Evelyn turned sixteen, I was only fourteen and a half. But we had such a special bond that she waited until I was fifteen, at which time I was able to convince my mother to bend her dating rule a little for me. She drew the line, however, on me going out with boys alone, and so double-dating with Evelyn became the standard routine.

After Evelyn finished high school, she got married and left home. I felt alone. It seemed to me as though she had left me behind and it saddened me to know that I wouldn't see her every day. Mother meanwhile, maintained her strictness on the subject of dating boys. Past the age of sixteen, I could go on a date alone, but I was required to be home by 10:00 p.m. And getting home early didn't win me any points. If I got home at 9:00 p.m., for example, I wasn't allowed to sit in the car with my date. I tested the rule once, and only once. One fine night I sat outside in my date's car, having noticed all the house lights off and assuming Mother was asleep. Bad assumption. Suddenly I saw her coming out of the house, running towards us, wielding her big straw kitchen broom. I got out of the car, completely and totally embarrassed, while the young man in question took off, never to ask me out on a date again.

Mae's husband, James McEfee, was about six feet tall and was very light complexioned. He had a good blue-collar job, one of the best in the county. Unfortunately, he also had a problem with alcohol, and when he wasn't working, he was drunk. Alcohol affects people differently. Some people who drink, whether moderately or excessively, get overly friendly. Others become mean. Alcohol can turn an introvert into an extrovert, a person of reason into a madman, and a gentle soul into a raving monster. James fell into the last category. When he'd have too much to drink, he'd become violent and mean. Not one to be pushed around, Mae got mean right along with the drunken James and they were always arguing and fighting.

The children saw what was going on, but there wasn't anything they could do about it. They needed as much a respite from the ugly, tumultuous atmosphere of their parents' house as we needed from all the tiring work we did all year round. And so they would be glad to come to their grandmother's to visit us and I would be so glad to have them there to play with.

One fall afternoon in 1954, when I was about eight years old, I was outside and I heard my mother screaming and crying from the house. I ran inside where she informed me that Mae had contracted tuberculosis. At that time I knew nothing about tuberculosis, but I could sense its seriousness from my mother's reaction. Although Mae lived in the city of Arkadelphia, she frequently had visited our home and we had been in her home as well. And so when she took sick, all of her children and all of us, too, had to have shots.

Although TB was becoming more and more understood by medical science, it was still greatly feared by many. People would panic if a neighbor was discovered to have contracted TB and in small towns like Arkadelphia, the panic often led to rash and grossly unwarranted action. To assure themselves the affliction would not spread beyond Mae's house alone, the city burned the house down. It was all her husband James needed as a reason to leave. Having spent most of his time fighting with Mae, he took the opportunity to now abandon her and their six children. He moved to St. Louis where his mother lived.

We never saw James again, nor did we ever care to. We didn't much care what the problems were between him and Mae; all we knew was that he ran out on her in her biggest time of need. It wasn't right to treat our sister in such a way and it made it difficult to ever think of James in a good way again. How, we wondered, could Mae have even ended up with such a man? But the matters of the heart remain mysterious.

Who knows what brings two people together? It wasn't ours to judge. Our duty was to be there for Mae.

Mae was hospitalized, quarantined, as was the case at the time with those stricken with TB. I remember the hospital where they took Mae was secluded up on a hill. The town was Alexander, Arkansas, about sixty miles from where we lived. We would go to see Mae whenever we could do so. Father sometimes would take us in his truck, and sometimes Mother would get Abraham to drive us. For us younger kids, it was a treat to go anywhere, even if it was a hospital sixty miles away. I remember the building made a great impression on me. It was so large that I imagined it was a city.

Amazingly, Mae slowly began to get better. After two long years of medical treatments, Mae beat the disease. She no longer had a persistent cough. We considered it something of a miracle, not that people couldn't recover from TB; there were treatments available that, although relatively new at the time, had begun to show significant success. But Mae's condition seemed, to us, to be dire. It was difficult, try as we might, not to find ourselves often fearing the worst, believing that Mae would most certainly not be able to fight through the illness. I think on some level, we had all prepared ourselves for the worst. And yet, Mae beat the odds. Slowly, but surely, Mae recovered completely.

But then came some decisions. Where would Mae go? What would she do? She had no home and she had no job. Fortunately, she had made friends with the hospital staff and had been offered a job as a cook in the hospital cafeteria. She took it, renting a room in a boarding house about five blocks from the hospital so she could walk to work. Mae was happy to be free of the disease and was excited to start a brand new life. Mother, meanwhile, kept Mae's children, and Mae would come to see them when she could. When she couldn't visit, she let the children know she cared for them by sending them money, which Mother used for household expenses and for the care of all the children.

Then, just four years later, tragically, ironically – after successfully defeating the mortal danger of tuberculosis – Annie Mae was dead. Apparently, after eating some leftover hospital food that had been used and reused, Mae contracted food poisoning. She fell ill quickly, but managed to hide it from Mother when Mother went to visit her. "I'm fine," she assured Mother, but she died within a week. It was a painful death and a senseless one. Today, of course, there no doubt would have been an investigation and a lawsuit. But in June of 1962, times were different. We simply didn't know any better. Mae was dead, we were devastated, and that was just the way it was. After her death, Mae's children got a small check, and that was a big help for the family.

Mae had six children when she was hospitalized with TB, ranging from one-and-a-half years old to ten. My mother had taken them in and raised them as if they were her own. While working in the hospital, Mae had met a man and ultimately had had two more children. We never met the new man. My mother took these children in, also, and raised all eight – five girls and three boys. Father resisted the idea of taking the children in, but when Mae died they had nowhere else to go. All of us lived in the nine-room house that Father had built and the additional kids were raised as if they were our brothers and sisters. No one was treated any differently than any other.

## SAMUEL

My brother, first-born son Samuel, left home before I was born. Growing up, Annie Mae called Samuel "Bud" and he called her "Big Sister." Eula Mae, born after Samuel, he called "Little Sister." This was their special way of distinguishing who was the oldest and who was the youngest of the three of them. Samuel had fourteen children and they all called him "Wee Daddy." His oldest child, my niece, is the same age as I am.

Samuel worked as a heavy equipment operator for the Missouri Pacific Railroad for fifteen years. After Union Pacific bought out

Missouri Pacific, he continued to work for the rail giant until he retired. It was hard work that frequently kept him away from home. He would come home on the weekends to do what he loved most, which was preach in his church. Samuel worked hard to build his own church, and his Sunday congregations were filled with family and friends. He died at the age of seventy.

## EULA MAE

Eula was the third child and she, too, left home before I was born. She had tried it once before, but hadn't gone far. As a young girl, having been beaten by Father like the rest of us would be, she once ran away. But with nowhere else to go, she decided to make the attic her temporary refuge. She stayed up there for three days, completely unnoticed. Mae was the only one who knew she was there, her confidante, fixing her food and bringing it to her. Eula would wait until Mother and Father weren't around, then come down to use the outside bathroom. Father, meanwhile, was terrified that Eula would never come home and that he would never see her again. He went out looking for her, searching everywhere. Eventually Eula came down from the attic much to Father's relief.

The incident was probably not surprising, given Eula's bullheadedness. She definitely had a mind of her own. At fourteen, she decided she was going to take up chewing tobacco. This, of course, was strictly forbidden in our father's house. Eula tried chewing in secret, or at least what she imagined was secret. One day Mother spied her chewing and demanded that she stop. Eula refused. And so Mother allowed her to continue chewing. The problem for Eula was that Mother wouldn't let her spit the tobacco out. She had no choice but to swallow the bitter liquid that had filled her mouth, causing her to very quickly become ill. It was the last time she ever chewed tobacco. When she got older she thanked Mother for taking the habit, and the desire, away from her.

Eula had a dark smooth complexion and coal black hair. She was uncommonly beautiful, prompting constant jealousy from Edward, the suitor who would eventually become her husband. Edward insisted on keeping his eye on her at all times. He kept Eula from doing some of the things she really wanted to do and by the time their seventh child was born, she had had enough. Eula got a divorce and tried to move on with her life.

Eventually she met Sam, who was twenty years her senior. Sam adored Eula and he made her happy. She bore Sam two children, but, in time, her happiness waned. After Sam died she decided she had had her fill of men and chose to remain unmarried for the rest of her life.

Eula was different than the rest of us. She didn't hesitate to speak her mind. She was demanding, and preferred to be in control. I remember that whenever we all got together, Eula would insist that because she was one of the oldest children, she should always get her way. I suppose she might have been the most like our father – not an easy person to live with. And she would frequently beat her children, some of whom turned out to be outstanding and some of whom seemed constantly to be in trouble. We thought of Eula as a character right out of an old Western; she enjoyed a good fight and she frequently carried a gun. Eula Mae was not a woman to be trifled with.

Later in her life she owned and operated a store in town called "What Not and What Every," where she sold literally whatever anyone needed – clothes, dry food, pots and pans, appliances, and seemingly everything else. The store was quite successful, the kind of entrepreneurial operation that Father would have been proud of. When she wasn't busy with the store, she was busy making quilts, something she seemed to be naturally gifted at. She gave each one of her sisters one of her special quilts.

About five years before Eula died, she became a Christian. She began to attend church regularly and became a different person, very likeable and much more enjoyable to be around. After I had opened my factory, I gave her some scraps of fabric that had gone unused. The scraps were all of various colors and at first glance didn't appear to complement each other at all. But I was overcome with joy when Eula presented to me one of her specially stitched patchwork quilts, with those same mismatched pieces of colorful fabric woven into it. I suppose a lot of people would look at this wildly colorful quilt and not find it especially pleasing to the eye, but I loved it, and still do. Not just for the gesture, but because I know it was made just for me by my sister during a wonderful time in her life, a time when she had become a much happier person.

## JAMES JR.

James, the fourth born, was named after my father. I saw him once in my life, when I was about seven years old. He had left the household, off to find work somewhere, and we were never to see him again. I remember Mother receiving a telegram one day informing her of his death. Details of the death were few and, being so young at the time, I don't really remember much more than just the telegram. As I got older I heard rumors. One rumor was that he had joined the Army and somehow met his death in the service. The other was that he had made his way to Florida where, one tragic night, he looked the wrong way at a white woman, was seized by a group of white men, and lynched.

I can't but help think we'd have had many more details of his death had it happened in the service. No Army representative ever contacted us, no uniform or personal belongings were ever returned to us. The lynching, though more dreadful to contem-plate than an Army death, actually seems more plausible, given the times. James wouldn't have been the first black man lynched for looking at a white woman. Nor would he be the last.

I remember the story of Emmett Till, a fourteen-year-old black boy from Chicago, visiting his relatives in Mississippi in 1955. At a grocery store, he reportedly said something flirtatious to the white woman who owned the store. She said something about it later to her husband. A few nights later, the husband and his half-brother grabbed Emmett right out of the house in which he was staying with his uncle, drove him to a remote barn and beat him to death, gouging an eye out in the process. They dumped his body in a river where it was discovered days later. The gruesome nature of the heinous crime made front-page news and for the first time, people around the country began to see how it really was that blacks were thought of by many of the whites in the south. The incident stoked the embers of the civil rights movement, fanning it into the flames of action. Emmett Till became a symbol.

As for James, we'll most likely never really know the truth of what became of him, but I can't help think, simply by the suspicious lack of details, that the rumors of a death by lynching were probably based on fact.

## Andy (Andrew) and Amos

Twins Andy and Amos were born on February 26, 1931. Andy was born at 1:00 a.m. and Amos followed at 1:30 a.m. Though their personalities were very different, the twin brothers' lives ended in the same tragic way.

Andy left home when I was about four years old. He married a woman who had five children and then they had five children together. They eventually went their separate ways, with all the children remaining with their mother. The more handsome of the twins, Andy was married three times.

Unable to read or write, Andy struggled throughout his life. He tried to open a restaurant once but was unsuccessful. He had a hard time coping with his struggles and fought a lifelong battle with depression. His life provided me with a first-person view of how depression can destroy a person's spirit. I would become a sounding board and confidant for Andy.

Occasionally, he would borrow money from me, paying me back sometimes, and sometimes not. He would call me or come to my home many times, just to talk. I would sit quietly and listen as he opened up to me about whatever was on his mind – his wife, one of his lady friends, or maybe just life in general. Often he would leave my home with tears in his eyes. I never questioned him about it; I knew he didn't want his sister to see him crying.

For a period of time, Andy became obsessed with a television evangelist and started sending him money. I didn't understand it then but I have since come to realize that, in some way, this helped Andy feel connected to the world. On the outside Andy looked happy, but I knew that on the inside he was a very lonely person, alienated from his fellow man. Perhaps the connection to the televangelist, indefinite though it might have been, made him feel less so.

One day, while I was interviewing potential employees at my company, I got a call to go right away to the hospital in Little Rock. I left immediately, picking up my sister on the way. Andy was in intensive care. He had been shot in his home. So had a lady friend who had been visiting him. She had died instantly. Andy was hanging on, unconscious, and would do so for another day. On June 14, 1989, he died.

We still don't know what happened in his house that night. And the murderer has never been caught. Oddly, seven years later, an eerily coincidental fate would fall upon Amos, Andy's twin brother.

## AMOS

On October 10, 1996, I received a call at my office that was similar to the one I had taken seven years prior about Andy. This time it was Amos, found in his home with a gunshot wound to his head, along with a lady friend who had also been shot. The circumstances were the same almost to the last detail. But this time, both victims had died at the scene. When I got to Malvern, Arkansas, they had taken Amos's body out of the house and the police had taped off the crime scene. When we went to view his body we could see the bullet hole right in the middle of his head, above his eyes.

Though the circumstances of their deaths were similar, the lives of the two twins were remarkably different. Where Andy struggled with depression, Amos had a genuine love of life. Andy found it difficult to maintain steady employment, but Amos worked cheerfully for most of his life at a lumber yard, making a good living.

Amos was a mild-mannered young boy who rarely got into trouble. There was an incident when he was seventeen that could have ruined his life but thankfully did not. One day while walking through the fields, he shot and killed what he thought was a wild hog. It turned out that the hog wasn't wild but belonged to a local white man. My father offered to pay for the hog but the white man would not accept the offer, instead demanding that the sheriff put Amos in jail. Amos was sent to the Arkansas State Prison without a trial. He stayed locked up there for six months. This was during the 1940s. Racism was prevalent, and it was common for blacks in the south to receive unfair trials or be denied due process under the law. With a choice of payment for his hog, or putting Amos – a black man – behind bars, the white man chose the latter. Father was infuriated, but there was nothing we could do. It was hard on all of us, but we prayed and we pulled together and survived it. I'm sure it was equally hard on Amos, but he survived it too.

When Amos got out he was the same loving person he was before he went in, the horrific experience leaving him unchanged. Anybody knowing Amos would not have been surprised by this. Amos lived his life full of hope and enthusiasm. And he was a kind person. He could speak like a lion, but was gentle as a lamb. A good brother, who was always kind to me, Amos bought me my first car when I eventually went off to college.

I often wonder how it is that some people seem to be so blessed with enthusiasm and kindness, while others walk through life as if they're dragging an anchor behind them, always depressed, always doing things half-hearted, totally lacking in any real passion. Strangely, I've seen this within my own siblings, even between twins like Andy and Amos. And yet we were all raised generally the same under the same conditions. I think at some point it's up to each of us to find that passion. I believe that it comes from within. Too many people wait for life to make the first move, as if it's just going to drop off something to be enthused about right on the doorstep. I believe you have to find your passion and then you have to find the ways in which to follow it. Life has everything you need, but you have to uncover it yourself.

Amos was married four times. He had one child before he was married and one from his first marriage. He survived two of his wives, but the other two marriages ended in divorce.

After retiring from the lumber yard, Amos sold liquor of all kinds from his home to his friends. He knew it was dangerous but he felt as though he needed to do so to supplement his retirement. It wasn't illegal for him to sell alcohol from his home, but it was risky because of the kind of people it brought to the doorstep. It turned out to be one of his regular customers who crept into his house that fateful night, intending to rob Amos as he slept. Apparently, Amos awoke, startling the man who proceeded to shoot Amos dead.

Though Amos died before his time, I always felt, because of his zest for life, that Amos lived more fully than most people do who live till old age. I suppose that might be the biggest thing Amos and I had in common. Even in the face of hard times and setbacks, I have refused to remain down. Like Amos, I'm constantly looking to move forward and get back up after a fall. Amos never looked back, never spent a minute in self-pity or resentment, even after having been sent to the Arkansas State Prison.

It would have been, of course, completely understandable had he done so. The racism we faced was everywhere. I have faced it many times since and I face it still. But I have chosen to use it as fuel. Tell me I can't do something. Tell me I'm not worthy of something. Try to keep me down. Nothing is more motivating to me. Amos understood.

## ABRAHAM

Abraham was the seventh child. A very industrious, hard worker, even as a young man he could pick more cotton than the rest of the family. He could pick a bale of cotton in one day. As an adult, Abraham always had money and it seemed like he was driving a new car every year. And whenever he would buy a new one he would sometimes pass the older one to one of my brothers. Other times he would just pull it behind our home and park it. This happened over and over. When my husband and I ultimately came to own the land and wanted to build on it, we had to clean it up because it looked like a junk yard. We had at least twenty-five cars removed.

In the 1950s and '60s, Abraham owned his own wood-hauling business. His peers in the industry respected him. And in those days as a young man, Abraham seemed to have it all – lots of money and plenty of women. By all accounts, he was living the good life. Besides his cars, and his many women, he loved gambling, dice being his preferred game of chance.

He should have been a millionaire, but Abraham died poor. Mostly it was because of his lack of self-control with the fairer sex. He was a very good looking man, and frequently women chased him. He was married five times in his life and had seven children, four of whom were by women outside his marriages. My mother took in two of the children and raised them after their mother succumbed to cancer.

But I knew Abraham as a very kind-hearted man, always quick to want to help you out if you needed it. While still young, he assisted our mother by giving her money to buy groceries.

He was strong, too. It was sometimes ironic because he could also be overly-sensitive, even childish at times. But he had real physical strength, something I first became aware of during the summer of 1963 when the annual carnival came to Arkadelphia. It wasn't a big carnival but it did offer entertain-ment enough to foment excitement in children from all the surrounding counties who looked forward to its arrival every September. It was a special treat for us poor children who rarely had the chance to play and just be children, let alone ride ponies or delight in the sugary sweetness of cotton candy or an ice cream cone.

One year I went with Abraham, with Henry, Aaron, and Moses coming along as well. Of course there were plenty of games and chances to win prizes at the carnival, but you had to be lucky or have some real skill at shooting or tossing. Or, as in Abraham's case, it didn't hurt to just be flat out strong. A couple of his peers convinced him to try his hand at one of the more popular games designed to test a man's strength. Men who thought they had what it took would swing a hammer and try to raise a clacker to a bell that was situated on top of a pole about twenty feet high. I remember watching as Abraham swung the huge hammer over his head and brought it down with all his might on the lever that propelled the clacker upwards. It shot immediately up to the top of the pole where it struck the bell with tremendous force, producing a loud *ding*. Of course, Abraham was not the only man to accomplish this feat that day, but he was, as I recall, the only one to do it on the first try.

Topping that act, he also wrestled a big gorilla that day, holding him down while a man who worked with the act counted to ten. As you might imagine, the next day, Abraham was the talk of the town.

Abraham's strength may have provided good conversation for the locals, but for him his strength was his livelihood. It took amazing physical power and stamina to continually go through the motion of swinging an ax into the tough, uneasily yielding bark of large, thick trees. One fall afternoon in 2000, Abraham had been out working in the woods as usual. That night when he came home, his wife noticed that he was continually scratching his leg. A bug bite, he told her – an unavoidable hazard when you work outdoors for a living. But several days later, when Abraham awoke in the morning he felt a terrible pain in his joints. It was then that his wife noticed that the harmless insect bite on his leg had grown from the size of a pinhole to a rash the size of a saucer, and was swollen and red. She talked him into going to the doctor and the doctor diagnosed Lyme disease.

Lyme disease is spread by a particular kind of tick carried by animals like raccoons, squirrels, deer, and even horses. No doubt Abraham's bug bite was from such a tick. Incidents of the disease are common and if untreated the disease can cause serious neurological damage. The disease isn't fatal and if diagnosed soon enough, treatable with antibiotics with few last-ing effects. But by the time Abraham was diagnosed, the disease had begun to affect his internal organs. When he was released from the hospital, he was not the man that he once was.

Fighting the disease ultimately drained Abraham of his strength and he would never be the same. He was barely able to work three or four hours a day, if at all, whereas before he would work eight and nine-hour days. His health continued to deteriorate and eventually Abraham's kidneys failed. For four years he was on dialysis before finally succumbing to the effects of Lyme disease at the age of seventy-two.

## SILAS AND PAUL

Silas and Paul were the second set of twins and the eighth and ninth born respectively. Like Andy and Amos, Silas and Paul were about as different as night and day – even as children. Though far less dominant and confident than Paul, Silas had a wealth of talents, some of which got him in trouble as a youngster and as an adult.

He had a beautiful singing voice and would frequently sing as he picked cotton, although I don't remember hearing him sing on the few cotton harvest trips he went on with us before he left home. Mother used to tell the story of a white man who offered to buy Silas if mother was willing to sell him. Apparently, the man wanted to put Silas in the circus as part of some minstrel show act, a sideshow caricature, complete with painted lips and everything. Naturally, Mother said no. The man persisted. Mother would tell us the story, wondering aloud what took more nerve – the man's assumption that my mother didn't love her child enough to not put a price on him to sell to any man, or the assumption that a God-fearing woman would thrust her child into what Mother perceived to be the amoral life of an entertainer.

At any rate, Silas was, of course, never sold and, in fact, on one of those cotton trips, he met the love of his life and they soon got married. They remain so to this day, with one child. Silas is a minister, and doing very well for himself. It was a good direction for him to go, and one that wasn't necessarily assured. Silas had a little problem as an adult. It turns out he rather liked to take things that didn't belong to him. I remember it being said that Silas would steal white off of rice. He did it strictly for fun and he would often tell us the story of how he once stole an antenna from someone's house while they were watching TV. Fortunately, however, Silas changed, as people do.

## PAUL

Silas's twin, Paul, left home when I was about ten years old. He went to California where he met a woman and fell in love. They soon got married and had four children. Though he enjoyed life in California, he would come home to visit us every three or four years.

Tragedy befell Paul and his wife one day when one of his sons, Jerry, was shot and killed, having been mistaken for some-one else. Apparently he was in the wrong place at the wrong time. I never learned very much about the incident but the loss was devastating to Paul. He never got over it and his son's killer was never caught.

Paul called me frequently when he was in the hospital in California suffering with congestive heart failure. I called him the day before he died. He seemed short of breath and we didn't talk long. But we spoke about the last time he was home, how we enjoyed each other and couldn't wait until we saw each other again. His wife called me the next day to tell me that he had passed. He was sixty-seven. All the siblings went to California for the funeral and we have all missed him these many years.

## ISAAC

Isaac was the tenth child born and he died at birth. My mother and father were heartbroken. It happened in the winter after the family had returned from picking cotton. My mother would say that that particular pregnancy was very hard on her. She had pulled a cotton sack all the while that she was pregnant with Isaac and always believed it was that that caused her to lose the baby.

## JOSEPHINE

Josephine was named after my father's sister. She eloped when I was eleven, taking all of three dollars from our baby sister Ruth's piggy bank and taking off with her boyfriend Frank. While she was living with us, I remember that she loved to agitate. She told us younger kids that we all came out of the big stump that was left when my father cut down a tree that was too close to our house, and for the longest time we all thought babies came from that big stump.

Her job at home was to cook. She started preparing family meals at the age of eleven when Mother was working out in the fields. It was a background that would prove very important for Josephine later in life.

I remember our mother telling Josephine that her head was as hard as a goat's head. Josephine could be selfish and liked to tell everyone what to do. She loved having authority and often got others to do her work.

After she got married to Frank, she thought she had it all, and when we went to visit, it certainly seemed like a good marriage to us. They never had children and Josephine clung to her husband. But as I got to know Frank, I came to learn he was as selfish as Josephine ever was, if not more so. I suppose I shouldn't have been surprised when, after twenty or more years of marriage, the two divorced. The split seemed to change Josephine's life forever.

After the divorce Josephine joined a church, and all she could seem to talk about was how holy she was. Nobody wanted to be around her. But later in life she changed and we found our sister again. She'd come to visit and we'd lie in bed talking and reminiscing all night.

Josephine's cooking skills have provided her with plenty of opportunities in life. For the past twenty-five years she's worked for Texas Senator Kay Bailey Hutcheson, becoming an integral part of the Hutcheson family. The love between them is mutual. I've had the great pleasure of meeting Senator Hutcheson and her family on a number of occasions and it's easy to see why Josephine remains so enamored with them. They truly are special people.

## JOSEPH AND JACOB

Joseph and Jacob were twins, but just like the twins before them, they were significantly different than one another. Joseph believed in having a good time and was a heavy drinker. It's fair to say he never really grew up, never really made anything of himself, although he had a love of music and became skilled with the French horn. For the most part, he'd hop on trains and hobo around the country.

He did find a girl once, getting married and having two children, making me believe that maybe he was on the right track. But the marriage didn't last and shortly after his divorce, at the age of twenty-six, Joseph was killed in a car accident.

## JACOB

Jacob was somewhat shy and stayed home a lot more than his twin. He used to travel with us to pick cotton. Father would typically stay home in Arkansas and make sure one of the older brothers would lead us to Texas, Missouri, Arizona, or wherever else we could find work. Jacob was the one who took us when he became old enough. But when Joseph was killed, Jacob had a hard time with it. He left home shortly thereafter, at the tender age of fourteen. He moved to Dallas where he found work and, eventually, the girl who would become his wife. Several years later they moved to Detroit where they still live. They have four children and Jacob owns and operates a successful body shop.

## HENRY

My brother Henry was four years older than I, but we were always close as children, a closeness that never waned, even after he married and moved out of state. We'd frequently have long phone conversations. As I think about it, all of my brothers were special to me in one way or another. Each possessed some individual personality quirk or special talent that made life just a little more bearable as we were growing up, under the strain of living with an abusive father and the rigorous schedules of migrant cotton picking.

Henry's special talent was at putting things together. I remember him always building something. He once built a small structure out of tin that we played church in as children. It was a single room with a wooden door and a floor of wood planks. We always had a lot of fun in it.

Later in life Henry owned his own carpentry business, notwithstanding the fact that he could neither read nor write. He wasn't the type to let a handicap like that stop him. He hired people to do the paperwork and bookkeeping for him and, with their help, he made his business thrive, building homes and performing repair work.

Henry was married and had one child, my niece. Eventually he moved to Detroit where he was living when he suffered a stroke. Afterwards he found it hard to get around but he somehow managed for nearly a year. One winter morning, his nephew Johnny called to tell me he had found his uncle sitting in a chair. Henry had apparently had a heart attack during the night and passed away. He was forty-eight. We had his body brought back home so that he could be buried in the family cemetery in Arkansas.

## AARON

Even though Aaron and Henry were closest in age to me, the way in which they each treated me couldn't have been more different. As a little boy, Aaron became very jealous of his new little sisters when my twin and I were born. It seemed he didn't care too much for the idea of two new babies coming along so soon to take his place as the new center of attention. The way mother and some of the older surviving siblings used to tell the story, Aaron asked his other brothers and sisters if our mother was going to take us back, and when they replied no, Aaron became inconsolable. "I don't care! I don't care!" he sobbed over and over. But Aaron soon learned that mother could love him and the new baby girls equally and over time he eventually got used to the idea.

Aaron, as it happens, is part of the reason I don't like milk to this day. One of my chores as a girl was to help milk the cows, all of which had names. Big Ethel was the largest cow and produced the most milk. When Aaron was a boy, he liked to take an occasional drink from Ethel's teat as he was milking her, squeezing the teat so that the milk would go directly into his mouth. Somehow, the image of him doing that turned me against milk forever.

Aaron could often be a mischievous child, getting into things and trying to lie his way out. He once called our uncle a "big, fat husky fool" and got a whipping from my mother. I remember being shocked by this; Mother rarely struck any of her children. But it was a stupid thing for Aaron to have done. To us children, it didn't seem as though Aaron really used his head very much. He wasn't very patient, either. He'd lash out at you for the smallest mistake. Once when Aaron was teaching me how to drive, I mistook the gas pedal for the brake. Before I knew it, he had hit my foot with a large stick.

But people grow. And today Aaron is married with one child and a very successful transmission business in Dallas. Just another entrepreneur that came out of our household.

## MOSES

Moses and I grew up together. He was spoiled by his older brothers and they treated him like a king, telling him that he didn't have to work because they would take care of him. Well, Moses grew up to do just the opposite. He quit school and traveled from state to state, working and taking care of himself.

Moses married and had a child, but then divorced. About that time he started a wood-hauling business which has grown into one of the top wood-hauling businesses in Arkadelphia. He's since remarried, finding the love of his life.

*Moses Art BQ Grill.*

Although he never finished high school, Moses is a talented and gifted man. He built a shop behind his home on the acres that he inherited from our parents, and there he makes just about any-thing he wants to make. A real artist, Moses has handcrafted some of the most beautiful grills and iron statues I have ever seen.

## MARK

Like Isaac before him, Mark died at birth. And, like Isaac, my Mother's belief is that the loss came from the daily hard work she did while pregnant with him. His death was also in the winter after the family returned home from picking cotton. Mother tried to be careful, but was unable to prevent such a tragedy from befalling her a second time.

## Ruth

Ruth was the last sibling born. Seven years younger than me, we grew up in the same house along with many of the others. But because of our age difference, we kind of got lost around each other. We never shared much conversation and Ruth actually had much more in common with Susan, a niece who lived with us and who was about a year older than Ruth.

But over time, Ruth has become one of my favorite sisters. She's a very giving person, and kind-hearted. If she has a fault, it's that she's never very sure of herself. It causes her to procrastinate. But she's married with a wonderful and understanding husband.

I know because, along with Moses, Ruth and I have homes on the forty acres that we inherited from our parents. And so Ruth and I spend a lot of time together, calling each other daily and doing things for each other, and often going on trips together. It makes me feel like a mother hen at times to look after Ruth so closely, but then again she looks after me the same. Maybe that's why she's so fond of telling me that, although she's the youngest, I'm still the baby.

## Mary and Martha

My sister Mary and I were the last set of twins and were the only twin girls. My parents were very proud of both of us. My father said the prettiest one was his, and that was Mary, who was born first. Mary was beautiful. Although Mother dressed us alike, my father always thought Mary was the special one. Perhaps it was Father's preference for Mary that made my mother gravitate towards me as much as she did.

Even though times were hard, my father managed to bring home candy and ice cream for Mary and me each time he returned from trips into town or sales trips. We were the only two that Father brought special treats to. Aaron, of course, was always jealous, but the older siblings thought we were special, too. Growing up I never knew any different. I thought that was the way it was supposed to be. We were the youngest, after all, and that seemed to confer a certain specialness about us.

Each time Father came home, we would go into Mother and Father's bedroom, where no one was ever allowed. Father would put whatever he had brought us on a table beside the bed and there we would enjoy it. Several times a week we would await his return with excitement and listen at the window for the sound of his old Studebaker truck driving up. Sometimes our father would give us a treat by taking us for a ride in that old truck.

As Father's favorite, Mary could do no wrong. She often took advantage of her position with Father and would pick fights with me that she knew I had no chance of winning. I was told that from birth Mary always took control. When we were nursing, Mary would always push me aside and latch onto the breast from which I was feeding.

In January 1947, Mary got sick with a cold. She had a fever and was vomiting uncontrollably. My father was not at home, so Mother asked one of my brothers to ask one of our white neighbors to take Mary to the doctor. Claire Helms was a pleasant woman who was quick to answer my mother's request. We lived next to her for years and years. And although the differences between us were clear, neighborly courtesy ruled the relationship. There was a mutual respect, a respect that lasted until Claire's recent death in 2010. I was saddened to attend her funeral, but glad to have known her.

At the hospital, Mary lasted only a few hours. Her bad cold had turned into pneumonia. She died one day before our second birthday. And although I was only two, I remember Mary well. Because she was my twin, we had been close. It was like a part of me had died when she left this earth. I still sometimes go to the cemetery and stand beside her grave and talk to her, especially if something is on my mind that I just can't shake off.

For my father's part, he felt as though a part of him had died on that day as well. I suppose, in hindsight, Mary should have been taken to the doctor much earlier. But in those days, we just didn't go to the doctor. The first time I visited one was when I had my physical examination to enter into college.

In fact, that particular physical examination just about made me want to give up on doctors altogether. The doctor was an old, white doctor in the town, short and bald. Most of the black folks around town went to him, so he seemed the natural choice for my college physical. As a young girl who had never been to a doctor before, I had no idea what to expect, nor any notion of what was appropriate behavior or inappropriate behavior for a practicing physician. And so when the doctor did a thorough examination, using bare fingers instead of gloves, I said not a word, not knowing any better, even though something inside my gut made me feel as though what we was doing wasn't quite right. At the time, I was too young to say anything and, of course, very determined to go on to college. To do so, I needed the physical. Eventually, of course, I was to understand the doctor crossed a line, and it's troubling to think of how many poor, uneducated girls this doctor – long-since passed away – took advantage of in this way.

Although now, many years later, I trust most doctors, I still find myself second-guessing doctorly advice and questioning a diagnosis here and there. Now I'm not afraid of speaking up. Of course this might have come about regardless as I have a tendency to want to maintain control of situations in which I find myself, whether it be a business dealing or a health issue. I keep myself informed and I ask questions. Lots of them. Fortunately, my current doctor takes it all in stride, knowing that this particular patient isn't going to just go along with what she's told without a pretty thorough explanation. It's empowering to take control of one's own health.

At any rate, after Mary's death, I did not understand what had happened. For a long time, I thought my twin sister was just taking an unusually long nap. I waited and waited and she never did awaken. It was months before I knew she wasn't going to come back. I believed she was alive. When I looked in the mirror I thought I saw her. I would say, "Mama! There's Mary!" For the longest time, any little girl I saw on the street I thought was Mary.

Weeks after Mary's death, Father would still come home with two pieces of candy and two cups of ice cream. I can still remember often seeing him furtively wiping his face with a handkerchief. I was too young to understand that he was wiping away tears from his eyes, trying to be the strong man that he was, but dying a little inside with every thought of his beloved Mary. Meanwhile, Mother clung to me as if she were afraid I'd be snatched away quickly and tragically, too. The whole house seemed to moan and it was a long time before our house felt like a home again.

Perhaps nothing is as tragic as the death of a child. A life filled with potential, being stopped in its tracks before it gets the chance to truly flourish. It was, of course, more common back in those days. And it was even more so in rural areas like ours. Medical technology was not nearly as advanced as it is today, and what technology there was remained largely unavailable in the poor farming areas of the south. And yet, as common as it might have been, it was every bit as tragic, and every bit as heartbreaking.

Our lives were never the same after my sister's death. Where there were two there was now only one. Beyond the deep and terrible sadness we all felt, my father and mother were profoundly affected. I often wonder if Father's cruelty, acquired as a natural part of the cycle of cruelty into which he was born, was nonetheless stoked further by the cruelty that he perceived the universe had visited upon him with Mary's untimely death. Father was never the same and a streak of ugliness that dwelled within might well have grown a little uglier in the days and months that followed the loss of my twin sister.

## Mary and Martha

When we were born Mary was the larger one and the dominant one. I was so small mother's nipple would not fit into my mouth so mom would squeeze milk into a tiny spoon for about 2 or 3 months before I could get my small mouth around her nipple. Mary would suckle her breast and take the other one before I could suckle.

Growing up as a child I always felt inferior or less than others. I think it all started with my twin sister who made me feel she was the boss and the aggressive one and sometimes hostile. I miss her so much. As I write this it brings back memories. I loved her and she loved me.

## Growing Up

We had a sand pile in front of our house where my sister and I played every day. after my sister passed away and I could still remember playing in the sand where we played every day. I would draw my sister in the sand and draw clothes on her, and talk to her every day. Some say that you can't remember anything at the age of 2 YES, I CAN, and I will never forget. I will always feel she was and is a part of me.

I will never forget her. every little girl I saw whether she was black are white I thought she was Mary.

My father was a minister and he knew the Bible very well. He bought books and was always studying. he was very book smart. In 1943 father purchased 40 acres of land that had gone to the state for taxes. He paid $4.18 for the 40-acre plot. today that is hard to believe but I have the abstract and I will always keep it. It's my history from when father bought the 40 acres. And it shows every time we had to mortgage it and that was every year. Because every year we picking up and traveled to pick cotton to pay off the mortgage and that was every year cycle. What a life but.

## I AM STILL HERE

I still have remaining scars of picking cotton. My left should be lower than my right should no one notices but I know it because when I put on a blouse it always goes to my left side but being a fashion designer, I know how to compensate by a stitch here and a stitch there to keep it straight.

I remember eating my first slice of bread. It was a treat for me. I was so happy I looked at it, I smelled it, played with it, then I ate it, what a treat.

Father was very strict when something went wrong, we didn't get a whipping we were beaten. I remember putting my head threw a chair rail with my bottom out and father setting in the chair with a belt I couldn't move and my bottom was all his. I THINK THE REASON I WAS BEATEN SO BAD WAS BECAUSE MARY WAS FATHER'S HEART, SHE'S ONE AND ONLY AND UGLY MARTHA WAS LEFT. I think father loved me in his own way. I didn't know that I love him also until he had passed, then I realized how much I did love him and how much miss him.

## (I AM STILL HERE)

I got many beatings growing up it's unbelievable. I remember father had planted Irish potatoes now it was time to harvest them, I was told to walk behind the mule and father and I pick up the potato and put them in a pail. Mother called me to the house and told me to peel some potatoes for dinner yes mother and I left the garden and began to peel potatoes. Father said you didn't do what I asked you to do, yes father I tried to explain he would not listen so another beating, mother couldn't stop him but was furious.

One of my jobs was picking okra sometimes no matter how hard you looked you sometimes would leave one or two parts. father would check behind me and sometimes he would fine one or two parts. Father would get whatever he could find, like a fishing pole he beat me until it broke 1 time then 2 times and 3 times until nothing was left to beat with.

Another job, one day it was my turn to plow father's watermelon, we had a mule named Fred I was plowing and Fred decided to lie down on some of father's watermelon vines. I tried to make him get up and he just would not move. I came home crying because I knew what was going to happen. Fred had messed up father's watermelon vines. I AM STILL HERE.

Sometimes father would have us to kill a chicken. It was my job or my time to hold the chicken's head so my brother with a small axe could chop off the chicken's head. I was terrified I would close my eyes and I held on for dear life because I knew what was going to happing next a whipping from father so I was frighten by holding the chicken head and fear from father if it got away.

Growing up I was very shy I thought I was ugly my hair was short and nappy and kinky I hated school I was bullied my whole family was picked on. I remember one day when we had a hard rain the gravel road had flooded and we were the last family to be dropped off. The bus driver put my family off and we had to walk home, my sister held my hand the water was up to my neck I thought I was going to drown. We had to walk about 60 ft through water.

When I was in grade school every day the teacher had each student to stand and read in front of the class. when it was my turn, I was so scared that every time I would wet on myself. I remember in the spring riding the bus to school every morning all the girls would have their sweaters on, in the evening they had their sweater around my shoulder,

I thought it was so neat and I always wanted a sweater but mother couldn't afford to buy me one.

## MY SPECIAL PLACE

I had a special place on the 40 acres where I would go. I called it my serenity place where I would go to pray, cry and think. No one new about my special place. I had no idea that at age 34 we would build our second home on the 40 acres on my special place. Growing up they said I wouldn't make it.

## I AM STILL HERE

I don't regret the hard work in my life, I think it made me stronger, I am grateful, faithful and thankful. I can always see a vision on where I am going.

It's easy, and tempting, to want to assign blame to things beyond your control. Or, for that matter, to lament the fact that you have less control over life's often random nature than you at first think you have. Father was a man with a lot of pride, a man who, though poor and struggling along with most of the poor black men of that era in the south, liked to believe he was in charge of his destiny. That life could deal such a cruel and crippling blow to his convictions, must have been a difficult thing to come to terms with. And if life treated him so cruelly, perhaps on some level he felt it justified to return the cruelty in kind.

Sometimes the memory of my sister's death recalls a pain that is as fresh as if it happened just yesterday. As I grew older, it got easier. Father had made Mary and me a pair of red rocking chairs and we used to sit in those chairs side by side and rock all the time. We spent so much time in those chairs that when our mother would fix our food, she would bring it out of the kitchen to us on a platter. Mary ate on one end of a little matching wooden table positioned between our rockers and I ate on the other. Whenever mother served any kind of meat, Mary always ate hers heartily and then divided mine and devoured a portion of it also. For a long time, I could not even look at those little red rocking chairs or think of sitting in the one that had been mine.

I often wonder what it would have been like to have grown up with a twin. Though I am close to all my living brothers and sisters, a twin is a bond like no other. In just two years we had shared so much. What more might we have shared had we both made our way through life, supporting each other, loving each other, being there for each other? You see more of yourself in a twin than you see, perhaps, in anyone else, and maybe that explains the connection. And yet, strangely, I never saw a real physical similarity between Mary and I, and our personalities were markedly different as well. Still, there was something there...something palpable between the two of us, something that would make me come to understand that in some way, Mary would always be a part of me.

Today, however, the only remaining tangible thing I have of my twin sister is a single photograph. We didn't have money for pictures back then; nobody had a camera and a trip to a photo studio was beyond my parents' means. And so the only photograph I have is one that was taken on the last day I ever saw Mary – a picture of my sister lying peacefully in her casket, beautiful as ever.

# CHAPTER SEVEN

# SCHOOL DAYS

*Martha wearing one of her early design.*

You might have heard the phrase "cut on the bias" but never knew exactly what that meant. Well, in sewing, a bias is simply any diagonal line that runs across woven fabric. For some people, it's very important to wear clothing stitched of fabric that was cut along a bias. Because fabric cut in this manner gives you the most stretch, clothing made this way tends to drape beautifully on a person's shape. If someone asked me how well my life fit me today, I might say "like a dress cut on the bias." This was not always so.

> *For much of my early life, I had to exhibit a lot of the "stretch" of bias-cut fabric; but it was awhile before I got to enjoy the "beautiful drape."*

I started school in the winter of 1951 when I was six years old. A married couple, Ann and Willie Taylor, taught all eight of the grades at the school, with Mrs. Taylor teaching grades one through four in one of the school's two rooms, and Mr. Taylor teaching grades five through eight in the other. The school had maybe fifty students in each room, each of them progressing at whatever level was appropriate. Second graders would be doing second-grade work out of their textbooks while Mrs. Taylor may have been going over third-grade material with the third-graders. Somehow the Taylors managed to make it work. But not in any kind of way we appreciated. The Taylors, to be blunt, were mean and cruel.

Mrs. Taylor was a petite woman with short, brown hair. But her threatening demeanor belied her small stature. Mr. Taylor, on the other hand, was slender and dark skinned, but nearly six feet tall, towering menacingly over the children in his room. Together, their strictness and meanness made it hard for many children, including me, to learn. I was afraid of them. And I had reason to be. The Taylors had short tempers and did not let a mistake, however slight, go unpunished.

All the girls who attended the school were required to bring pocket handkerchiefs with them. One day I forgot mine and was made to stand in a corner on one leg for two hours. I remember being so afraid to ask the teacher to use the outside bathroom that I just relieved myself right there. This happened on a number of occasions until my mother grew tired of me coming home in soiled clothing. Then I was faced with my choice of ire from Mother or the Taylors, neither of which was enjoyable.

The school was a rural school, fifteen miles from where we lived. It was an old, unpainted wooden building with floors made of unfinished planks. We took our lunch to school in brown paper bags, typically with a biscuit filled with syrup or the jelly Mother sometimes made. Often times we had very little to eat.

Most children were aware of the Taylors's reputation as strict and unrelenting disciplinarians years before they were faced with their first day at the schoolhouse. Unofficially, children were expected to know and obey the rules of the schoolhouse on the first day or be prepared to pay the consequences for breaking them. My brother Moses never knew the rules. And on his first day of school, he walked happily and excitedly inside with his cap still on his head. Moses paid little attention to Mr. Taylor who called out behind the happy lad, "Cap." Moses kept walking, oblivious in his excitement about starting school. Mr. Taylor said again, "Cap." Again, Moses kept walking. This time Mr. Taylor took his oak stick and hit Moses on the head. Moses began to cry, but at least he did remove his cap.

Mr. and Mrs. Taylor took discipline and punishment into their own hands and never told our parents. Even if they had, it would not have made any difference. Father was too busy to even notice what went on at school, and Mother, although concerned, was powerless to do much of anything.

Of course being as young as I was, it never occurred to me that this was not the way a school should be. It was just the way it was. But I hated every bit of it. The days were long as we had to leave for school every morning around 7:00 a.m. and wouldn't get back until after 4:00 p.m. I remember sleeping on the bus, I'd be so exhausted. And the daily experiences with the Taylors made me – already severely introverted – even more shy and reticent. I was afraid to say even a word. Unfortunately, my silence was misdiagnosed as slowness and I was forced to repeat the second grade, making my life with the mean Mrs. Taylor longer by a year. It was extremely difficult for me to handle the idea that I was being held back while the rest of my classmates were going on to the third grade. Of course when you're a mere second-grader, you don't much argue and fuss about your lot in life. You accept it. Not that my pleas would have found much sympathy with either Mrs. Taylor or my parents.

Going through the second grade twice provided plenty of memorable events, but few as comically odd as what happened the day my mother gave me an apple to carry in my lunch. We rarely had apples to carry in our lunches and I was delighted to have such a special treat. I happily ate the apple peel first, but was startled to find that one of the other kids had been watch-ing me the whole time. She looked at me strangely and told me that the apple was no longer good since the peel was gone and that I should give it to her. My shyness bound my tongue, but even if it hadn't, I was so confounded by what she had said that all I could do was stare at her quietly as I continued to devour my precious apple until it was all gone.

Getting held back was yet another example of a difficulty I faced early in life. One wonders at why some children never seem to get over early problems while others seem to use them as fuel for later in life, fuel they use to grow and become strong. How often do we hear of people using a difficult childhood as an excuse for problems in adulthood? I suppose it's possible that the challenges I faced early could have defeated me, could have made me want to easily surrender to "the fate" that was mine from childhood. By the grace of God, for some reason, my challenges have only served to inspire me to rise above them.

Our farm was located in a part of the district that was gerrymandered. As a result, we couldn't ride the bus with the local white children, and were unable to attend the all black school that was a mere six miles from our farm. After Mr. and Mrs. Taylor's school closed, when I was in third grade, we had to climb onto a bus daily and travel seventeen and a half miles to Henry Bell Elementary School in Gurdon. The elementary, junior, and high schools were all on the same grounds, but were housed in separate buildings. The Bell schools accommodated black children from the town of Gurdon, which had a population of about 5,000 at the time, as well as surrounding areas like South Central.

It was a long ride to and from school, and I remember that sometimes when it would rain the dirt roads would flood, becoming streams of mud. As the bus couldn't go through the flooded roads, the driver would stop and put us off. We'd have to walk home through knee-high mud, or worse. I remember Josephine holding my hand as we walked so that the current, often coming up to my shoulders in areas, wouldn't sweep me away.

It happened that the Taylors' daughter worked at this school and although she ultimately turned out to be a very nice lady, at the time she seemed pretty fond of making use of her parents' method of enforcing discipline. One of her techniques was humiliation, and she especially liked to humiliate us Smith kids. Being dirt poor I suppose we were easy targets. In addition to school we had to go to work every day to help support the household. If it wasn't picking cotton, it was some other form of cheap labor work. My brothers would cut logs and haul billets, often missing a day or two of school here and there for the work, always to be verbally humiliated in front of the rest of the kids when they returned. And of course if the humiliation is coming from a teacher, it's not hard to imagine that it gets picked up pretty quickly by the other children. We'd get it from all directions, and naturally none of that was doing anything to help me get over my shyness.

Mostly we'd be made fun of for our work in the cotton fields. I had started picking cotton when I was old enough to carry a gallon pail. I would fill it with cotton and empty it into my mother's sack. When I was about four years old, my mother stitched a small rope on each side of a burlap potato sack. I started with a twenty pound one and when I got older, it was increased to a fifty pound sack. At eight years old, I was dragging a four foot sack, and by the time I turned nine the sack was sometimes six or seven feet long, my quota four hundred pounds or more per day.

Because my brothers and sisters and I traveled with our parents to harvest cotton, we started school later than the other children. By the time we all started school in January, our skin would be two shades darker because we'd spent the waning summer and early fall months baking in the sun picking cotton. The other children would taunt us, calling us "tar babies." The children would also make fun of our hands because they would be so rough from picking cotton. "Reptile hands," they would call them. Some of the teachers would join in the laughter with the other students, if they weren't actually instigating it themselves. We learned out of necessity how to fight and defend ourselves, but most of the time it was us who got into trouble, no matter who it was that may have started the fight.

I remember one of the older boys used to sit behind me on the bus every day, pulling my hair and thumping my head. All I could do was cry, because I knew if I told my parents they wouldn't do anything. Often I wished my older brothers were around to defend me, but they had all quit school by this time.

In the fourth grade, all the children were counting the vertebrae in my back one day, starting at my neck and contin-uing down to my waist. It was an old wives' tale that you could predict the number of children a girl would have by the numbe of vertebrae in her back. The children taunted me, saying that because so many bones were present in my back, I was going to have as many as twenty to thirty children.

The teachers at Bell Elementary School took discipline and punishment into their own hands – much like the Taylors – and rarely told the parents of the students when there was trouble. When it came to me and my brothers and sisters, the teachers really didn't have an opportunity to tell our parents even if they wanted to because Mother and Father never came to school for any reason. Consequently, they were never there to defend us against the abusiveness of our school peers and the teachers. Our teachers came to believe our parents didn't care about us and so they treated us even worse. I sometimes think it's a wonder that we didn't come to believe that we were simply not worth protecting.

The fact is, the Smiths just weren't very well liked. A lot of that animosity came about on account of my father. James Smith had the audacity to stick up for himself, whether it was to a black man or a white man. He stood his ground and people didn't always appreciate it. And as cruel as he could be to us kids, he stood up for us against others as well, around the house, at least, if not at school. One of my sisters was walking home one day when she was offered a ride from a neighbor, but when his car arrived at our house, he just kept driving, towards the woods. His intentions were pretty plain to my sister who jumped out of the car at the first opportunity, running through the woods as fast as she could. The neighbor got out of the car and chased her, trying to keep up, looking for her bright, white blouse through the dark and heavy trees. Wisely, she took the blouse off as she was running. He lost her in the woods and she doubled back towards our house, showing up naked from the waist up, scratches all over her legs, and completely out of breath.

There was no hiding what had almost happened, of course, and Father didn't exactly take kindly to somebody trying to take advantage of one of his own. The neighbor actually skipped town for a couple months, hoping no doubt that things would blow over. They didn't. When he returned, Father hadn't exactly gotten over his fury. When the neighbor happened to drive past, Father grabbed his gun and chased him in his truck, taking pot shots at him until the neighbor finally drove out of sight. To this day I don't imagine my father's intention was really to shoot the man. I'd like to think those were just warning shots that he was firing. Of course with Father, one never really knew. Either way, he had a reputation as a man not to trifle with. That made people uncomfortable and that discomfort manifested itself as abuse often directed at us kids.

It also didn't help that most of the other black families around seemed to be kin to one another. We didn't appear to be kin to anybody. That changed, of course, upon my success when it suddenly seemed like everybody I knew was some long-lost cousin. If not cousin, at least some "best" friend from way back. Funny how that happens with success. I guess they all forgot how they treated the shy little homely girl who picked cotton.

I do remember, however, that there were a couple of teachers that sympathized with us and really tried to help. Two that I remember in particular were Mr. Henry Bell, Jr., our history teacher and whose father the school was named for, and Mrs. Wilson, my junior high home economics teacher.

Mrs. Wilson was impressed with what I knew about sewing and pattern-making, and she would ask me to help all the other students. Most of the time she would just leave the classroom, confident that I knew how to answer any questions from the class as long as the questions were about sewing. Needless to say I really enjoyed Mrs. Wilson's classes and she was a great source of encouragement for me. When you're young and impressionable, the least little comment can make a difference. A discouraging word can wound you and an encouraging word can raise you up. Mrs. Wilson's encouragement was a lifesaver in a sea of often-discouraging treatment by other students, and, sadly, by other teachers as well.

My head start in sewing came from home where I had a lot of practice, especially since I practically clothed my entire family. Home economics gave me the opportunity to demonstrate my natural talent for dress making. It was a gift I'd discovered early when at the age of eight I made my first dress, by hand and on the machine that mother used to teach us on. I cut the patterns from paper bags and my mother let me use her old treadle machine to sew it. Soon I was making my own clothes as well as clothes for some of my brothers.

Over time, my gift became a great blessing to the entire family. Because we were so poor, our parents could hardly afford to buy new clothes for their rapidly growing children. My time at the sewing machine was literally the way our parents put clothes on our backs for a long while.

I think that at one point it must have been Mother's intention to teach all of her girls the important skill of clothes making and mending. This was the reason she purchased the machine in the first place. It was an old tread sewing machine that you had to power with your feet by pushing down on floor pedals. Mother tried to teach Josephine but Josephine couldn't get the machine to do anything but go backwards. She'd get so frustrated that she'd cry and Mother would show her again, hoping desperately that after a little more coaching, her child could at least get the stitch going straight. After countless tries and what seemed like hours on that machine laboring over a piece of fabric and fighting with the floor pedals for control of the needle, Josephine would finally tire of trying. Mother of course knew there was little point in trying to teach an unwilling and discouraged pupil. After that, whenever anyone in the family needed any sewing done, they asked me or Mother to do the job. To this day, Josephine can't so much as sew on a button. But of course she had a much better time of it in the kitchen. Strange how people have different talents. Each of us has made the best of ours.

But outside of Mrs. Wilson's home economics class, things were tough. We had to buy our own books in junior high and I remember buying some of my white neighbor's books, since we were in the same grade. Unfortunately, when I got to school that year, it turned out my books were the wrong ones. Yes, we were in the same grade, but my neighbor's books were a year ahead of what I needed. That's the way it was for me most of the time. I was always so far behind in my studies that one night, in complete desperation, I put my books under my pillow and prayed that the information would leave the book and soak into my head. Of course it never did.

Compounding my problems was my bashfulness. It prevented me from speaking up when I had trouble at school, whether it was with my work or my teachers. And I never considered myself attractive. In fact, I thought I was homely. No matter how hard I tried to make my hair look right, it just never worked out. And I was small, much smaller than the rest of my siblings.

It wasn't until I was in eleventh grade that I finally began to come out of my shell. It was only then when my family stopped working in the cotton fields. Finally I was shed of the embarrassment of being a cotton picker. My hands were no longer torn up and nobody could any longer tell at a glance what menial labor my family and I had been relegated to.

At about the same time, I overheard a twelfth grade girl, Gurtherine Lewis, talking to her sister, a classmate of mine by the name of Shirley Lewis. Gurtherine was talking about me. "She's a nice-looking girl," the twelfth grade girl had said. Nobody had ever said that about me before. For the first time in my life it occurred to me that maybe I wasn't so ugly after all. It boosted my confidence. Again, a simple encouraging word, said at an impressionable age, would make a difference. From that point on, my bashfulness slowly began to recede.

# PHOTO GALLERY

*Martha and Huie Dixon*

# HUIE AND CHRISTOPHER
## MARTHA'S FAMILY

*Christopher's
Kindergarten Graduation*

*Kindergarten Graduation
at Gurdon School*

*First year at
Arkadelphia School
Third Grade*

*Huie and Christopher
wearing suits that Martha
had designed.*

# HUIE AND MARTHA'S HOME

*Martha reading while sitting on her deck.*

*Driveway gate of Dixon family home.*

*Japanese garden.*

# MARTHA'S ORIGINAL DESIGNS

*Martha wearing one of her own design, 1986.*

*Martha wearing her early designs.*

# GOWN DESIGNER
## DESIGNER FOR A FIRST LADY

*Martha showing her design sketch of the Presidential Gala Gown.*

*The Governor's Inau*

*The Presidential Gala Gown. 1992*

# DIXON MANUFACTURING
## PROGRESSION OF A COMPANY

*Original building in 1866*

*Dixon Manufacturing, 1988.*

*Dixon Manufacturing, DMI Factory Outlet and Martha's Design, 2006.*

# INSIDE DIXON MANUFACTURING

*Inside Dixon MFG, 6-5-1997.*

*Courtesy of Daily Shiftings Herald.*

*Christopher draws a pattern for Tyson Company. "The Pattern Process" Aug 12, 1996.*

*Inside Dixon MFG, 11-16-1999.*

*Nursing uniforms.*

# INSIDE DIXON MANUFACTURING

*Martha at a show in Dallas, TX., 1999.*

*Sewing Nursing uniforms.*

*Sewing Tyson uniforms.*

*Nursing uniforms.*

# AWFL VISITS DIXON MANUFACTURING

*AWFL visits and observes the process at the Dixon Manufacturing plant.*

*AWFL visits Martha's manufacturing plant.*

*AWFL function at Martha's home.*

# THE ARKANSAS BLACK HALL OF FAME

*Inducted into the Arkansas Black Hall of Fame, 2005.*

*Huie and Martha at the Arkansas Black Hall of Fame, 2005.*

*The Arkansas Black Hall of Fame.*

AR Black Hall of Fame photos courtesy of Jorden Davie Photography.

*Inductees, The AR Black Hall of Fame.*

# AWARD RECIPIENT

*Recipient of the 1995 NAACP Executive Award.*

*Recipient of the 2004
Business Professional
Women of Arkansas Award*

# SOUTHERN WOMEN IN PUBLIC SERVICE

*Talking with Janet Reno,
Southern Women in Public Service.*

*Southern Women in Public Service.*

# CAMPAIGN TRAIL

*Little Rock Democrat Party Function.*

*Democrat Party Function with President Clinton, 1995.*

*Little Rock Democrat Party Function.*

*Atending an Al Gore function.*

# CAMPAIGN TRAIL

*Campaign for President Clinton/Vice President Al Gore in Alabama, 1991.*

*R. Slater, V. Morgan, Martha Dixon, Rodney Slater and President Clinton.*

*Martha Dixon and Hillary Clinton.*

*Martha Dixon and Jesse Jackson, Sr.*

*At a President Clinton function.*

*Martha Dixon, Tipper Gore and Senator Lincoln.*

# CAMPAIGN TRAIL

*Willie Brown in attendance at President Clinton function, 1997.*

*Jimmie Lou Fisher 2000 campaign for Governor.*

*Democratic function, 1997.*

*Democratic function, 1998.*

*At a democrat function with Rodney Slater, US Secretary of Transportation.*

# CAMPAIGN TRAIL

*Martha and son, Christopher Presidents Ball, 1996.*

*Standing with Carolyn Huber, the White House hostess.*

*Martha standing in the White House garden.*

# CHAPTER EIGHT

# MAKING MY OWN WAY

## Guarding the Straight Grain Line

*If you've ever set out to make a dress or suit or gone to a seamstress or tailor to have a dress or suit made, then you probably have used or bought commercially packaged paper patterns. The pattern is simply a large sheet of paper, imprinted with lines that guide the seamstress as she sews the dress or blouse or whatever item of clothing she is endeavoring to create. The seamstress attaches the pieces of fabric to the pattern – usually with pins – along these lines, knowing that if she aligns them correctly she will end up with a perfect dress, skirt, or blouse. All of the lines on the pattern are important; none is more important than the straight grain line. A careful seamstress, therefore, is ever vigilant of the straight grain line. She knows that if she is to reach her goal of a beautiful dress, blouse, or skirt that will hang properly and flatter the figure, she must make sure the fabric is placed correctly on the pattern, particularly the straight grain line.*

On September 16 1960, my father died. He was fifty-seven. Although I was only fourteen years old at the time, I became the matriarch of the family. I took care of everything from tasks as simple as reading and writing to getting most of my siblings' birth certificates. I drove without a driver's license because whenever any member of the family got sick and needed to go to Little Rock to the doctor or to the hospital, it was I who had to take them. My mother could not read or write so she depended on me.

My mother had it hard after Father's death. My father hadn't earned enough money for my mother to draw from his accumulated social security funds, nor did he have any money to leave her. In order to survive, we had to continue to pick cotton.

The land my father owned went into heir property upon his death, which decreed that the land belonged to all the siblings. This meant that all the siblings would get an equal share – two acres each. No one sibling could build on their share or sell any of it without the knowledge or permission of the other siblings. Eventually, the family, including Mother, decided for simplicity sake, and for the sake of keeping the land together, to have it put all in one name. By then, having taken charge of most of the real responsibilities of the household, it was agreed that the land would be deeded over to me.

In the interim, with most of my older siblings having grown and moved on, some of the land had been turned back over to the state. The task fell to me to take care of the paperwork to get it all back, and to have it put in my name. All of fourteen years of age, I found myself having to set up an appointment to go see an attorney, which was intimidating to say the least. It was not only my first experience dealing with a lawyer, it was my first experience dealing in business matters with white people. I was scared to death. I remember walking up a daunting set of narrow steps in an old hotel where the law office was located. Everybody was nice to me when I came in. Maybe they sensed how scared this little girl was.

The legalities all seemed terribly complex to me, with terminology that might as well have been of a foreign tongue. And I was deathly afraid of asking a stupid question, betraying my ignorance, being humiliated. But the attorney explained everything to me simply, telling me what needed to be done, and making sure it happened. The business and legal world never seemed as scary to me after that. My confidence grew from the experience, as did the expectations of the rest of the family. My responsibilities to the household became greater.

I suppose my leadership abilities, which would serve me well throughout my life, were first established here. I felt the responsibility, and although it might have seemed intimidating at times, I also felt like I could handle whatever needed handling. Nobody else seemed prepared to step up, so I knew it was up to me. That gave me strength, and by taking care of some of the bigger responsibilities, I learned confidence, too. I came to trust in myself.

That's a huge thing. If you can't trust in yourself, if you don't believe in yourself to make the right choices and do the right things, then you're going to end up afraid of trying *any*thing. You'll live in fear of making a mistake. This kind of thinking can paralyze a person, rendering them impotent and incapable of any serious action. And so, in retrospect, although I might have felt burdened at the time, I look back now and I feel blessed that the important tasks of the day fell to me.

Things weren't always completely under my control, how-ever. In at least one respect, Mother was still very much in charge and I remember clearly the one time that I went against her will. On one of our cotton-picking excursions, when I was just fifteen, I met Birt Young, a twenty-one year old man who was, for whatever reason, sweet on me. I didn't really know anything about him and to this day I can't even say why I found myself drawn to him. As a teenage girl, the only important things were that he was an older man, and that he was paying attention to me. That's all a typical teenage girl requires, I suppose. Pretty quickly I was certain that I was in love.

Mother tried hard to discourage the relationship, and it became a real source of friction between us. I was sure I knew what I was doing. I was sure I knew what I was getting into. This man became my entire world and Mother just didn't understand.

Of course, a mother knows best. Birt wrote a hot check and went to jail for two years. I thought my heart would break. Naturally I would come to realize being apart from Birt was one of the best things that could have happened to me. I'm not sure I would have finished school with the distraction of a boyfriend, particularly one like Birt Young. And of course Mother knew all along that if I pursued the relationship with Birt, I might well have ended up marrying him and having children before I was ready for it.

I tried to help Birt as best I could prior to his sentencing. I went and saw a lawyer, one of the best defense attorneys in town, a well-respected, white man who had been practicing law for years and years. That Birt might have been guilty of what he'd been charged with certainly went through my mind. But when you're young and in love, you just don't look at things that way. I was sure there had to be some extenuating circumstance or some plausible reason why Birt was in trouble. And if I could just get this attorney man to take his case, justice would prevail and Birt would be returned to me.

Although it wasn't my first experience seeing a lawyer, I was still nervous. The defense attorney was an older man, smart, educated, white, and well-known in the community. He was an authority figure to me, the kind of person you put your trust in and whose advice you take unthinkingly, especially if you're a poor, black, fifteen-year-old girl.

The only problem was the advice I got from this man wasn't exactly the kind of advice I was looking for. As I sat across from him at his desk, wearing a sun dress, he rose, walked around behind my chair, and began to rub my bare shoulders. "You're very pretty, miss," he said. "Tell you what I'll do. Come around to my house tonight about 9:00. And I'll make sure to keep this Birt of yours out of jail." I tried to say something but the words got stuck and all I could do was stand up and walk directly out of the man's office. I went right home and found a place to be alone where I cried. I never told anybody until years later and never told my mother at all.

It was another case of an authority figure abusing his position, just like the doctor I went to see to get my college physical. In both cases I kept my mouth shut, either not knowing any better, or knowing that even if I was to say something, the word of a young girl wasn't going to go very far against the word of a long-time, well-respected member of the community. It was a no-win situation. And, just like with the doctor, I couldn't help but wonder how many other girls had been victimized by this attorney.

Birt, meanwhile, went away to serve his prison sentence. And though it would ultimately be for the best, all I knew at the time was heartbreak. I was crushed. There would never be another Birt Young, I was just certain of it. Depressed and feeling all alone, I went to the place I always went to when I needed to think and pray. It was a place behind our home on a grassy hill, a place that was all mine.

*Our meditation bench.*

All through my childhood it was where I always went. No one ever knew about my secret place. I spent many days sitting there, crying and praying about Birt Young, sitting in jail, taken from me. Mostly, of course, like any teenage girl with a broken heart, I just felt sorry for myself. But, like any teenage girl, I quickly forgot Birt when the next boy came along who paid attention to me.

Meanwhile, I continued with my schooling. It was still a struggle and would be throughout most of high school. But, with the grace of

God, and some hard work, I finally made it. I was the first one in my family to graduate from high school and attend college.

In time, Mother came to depend on me more and more. I took her to town to do her grocery shopping and took care of other things for her as well. All of the business that she needed to take care of, I was there to do it for her. I had leaned on Mother for so many years and when she could no longer do things for herself it seemed natural for me to step in and do as much as I could. Sometimes it seemed as if I was my mother's mother. And as I grew older, we grew closer to each other.

I eventually would build a house on the family property, where I could walk to Mother's house instead of driving the five miles where my previous residence had been. I could see her every day now. And there were times at night when I couldn't sleep and I would get out of bed and go to her house where we would sit up in her big bed together and talk for hours. Our relationship became one that most mothers and daughters might only dream of having.

In some sense, however, Mother would always remain strong and independent in her own way, even in those later years. She didn't really want anyone taking care of her, and she certainly felt as though she didn't *need* anyone to take care of her, either. I remember driving by her house one day and waving to her while she stood out front, chopping wood into small pieces that she would use in her old wood burning stove. To me, it looked like something out of the 1800s. But it was all Mother knew, and it was all she had a need of knowing.

This strength and independence is something I picked up from her. As with the qualities I picked up from my father, Mother's strength was nothing explicitly taught to me. Rather, Mother led by example. She provided a model of behavior that would influence me my whole life. Often times this character-istic becomes manifest in ways that I don't even notice. Other times, I see myself doing something or acting in some way that recalls the quiet strength of my mother, and I recognize it right away. "There's me, being just like Mother," I will find myself thinking.

One day in January, 1982, Mother called me and said that she was sick and asked me to take her to Twin Rivers Hospital. I drove her the several miles it took to get to this hospital, where the doctors determined that she'd had a mild stroke. I remember being in disbelief, because Mother hadn't complained to me about feeling sick at all. It seemed the stroke had not affected her speech, because she was able to tell me clearly that she wanted to go to the hospital that day. Because of her age and her medical history, they kept her a few days to make sure she was okay. Mother recuperated and progressed well and the doctors cleared her to go home in about three days.

The day she was to be released, however, she had another stroke. She was then transferred to Doctors Hospital in Little Rock. Before she left, I told her that I loved her and she told me she loved me. She never said another word. She was in the hospital at Little Rock for twelve days before she died. I was the only one with her when she took her last breath. When she died I was holding her hand. This was something that we had done many times. Sometimes when I would take her to town I would put my hand out and she would take it and we would squeeze each other's hand. This was the way we said "I love you."

Before my mother's death she had retained a lot of fluid. I remember when we went to the funeral home to view her body, seeing the imprint of my hand still on hers. She died on February 1, 1982 and was buried on February 5th, the same date on which my twin sister died and the same date she was buried just thirty-five years earlier. My mother was thirty-six years old when my twin sister and I were born and I was thirty-six years old when Mother died. In fact, Mother passed away the day before my thirty-sixth birthday; obviously it was not a happy birthday for me that year. I had a hard time dealing with it all and thought God was somehow trying to punish me. I felt alone and lost.

# CHAPTER NINE

# A FAMILY OF MY OWN

When my mother died, I couldn't eat for almost a week. I would lie on the floor in my bedroom every day and cry. Sleep was impossible. I was married by then, with a son, but the pain of my mother's death made it difficult to function as a wife and mother. My husband supported me by doing what he could, including taking care of our boy. My grief lasted months. I kept the change that Mother had in her purse when she died for five years. It took me that long to fully grieve.

My husband was Huie Dixon. I had met him in 1965 after my brother Abraham's wife had just died, leaving behind two children. I moved into their home to help care for their kids and Huie lived across the street. We actually met in church one summer night and started to see each other.

Huie worked at Henderson State University in the cafeteria as the head baker. I had just graduated from Peake High School and had started summer school at Henderson State. Huie and I got to see each other every day. After the summer I moved back home and we didn't see each other quite as much, but we continued dating for the next two years. We talked about getting married but couldn't afford it. I decided to drop out of school and got a job as a switch board operator with Southwestern Bell.

Finally, in 1967, we married, living with Huie's mother for about six months until we found a place to rent. Huie, mean-while, found another job at Arkla Gas. I started looking for a new job, too, and soon found one at Levi Strauss. We saved our money and four years later, in 1971, we built our first home.

The home we built was in Gum Springs, Arkansas, a small town where Huie had grown up. Gum Springs was about five miles from South Central where I grew up. Two years later, Huie and I adopted our son, Chris. I quit working and became a stay-at-home mom. Being a mother was very special to me; my family was complete. Even now my son and husband are everything to me.

After a few years in Gum Springs, we decided that our home was closer than we wanted to be to other homes in the community.

*Martha and Huie DIxon's home.*

We moved out further in the country and settled on twenty acres. Although all of the siblings had equal shares of our parents' land, the land that was now in my name, some weren't ever going to use it, having moved to Texas or California or Michi-gan. They offered to sell their shares to Huie and me, and we bought them. Now we had twenty more acres. Huie and I then decided to build our next home, in 1980, this one on the family property where I was born and raised.

Amazingly, without any hint from me, Huie would pick my special place – the grassy hill where I would go as a child to be alone – on which to build our second home. I sit out on my deck now, looking out at all God's beauty as I did growing up, sitting on the hill. I can see all that my father created, and I remain amazed at what he had done. The terraces that he had built on the land to keep the land from eroding are still here fifty years later. No doubt they will still be here long after my death.

At the time we built the house, Mother was still alive, and very excited that I would be so close. It gave her a chance to spoil her grandson. She made a wonderful grandmother, as loving to Chris as she was to any of her own children. The years living close to her were special, and she provided me with a lot of help and motherly advice during those first few years after we had adopted Chris. He was only five when she passed away and I often wish she had lived long enough to see the fine young man he has become. But, then again, I like to think she does see. She would also see the three-acre lake we have added to the property to honor her: Lake Beatrice.

*The lake on the Dixon's property was named Lake Beatrice in honor of Martha's mother.*

After Mother died, we rented out her house, the very house I had grown up in. We had split it into two units with the hopes of renting out the second half, as well. With the tenants out of the house one day, a small fire began. No one quite knows how – an electrical short, or maybe something left on the stove. But the small fire quickly grew. The fire department was summoned, but when you live as far out in the country as we did, summoning the fire depart-ment is nothing more than a mere formality.

Fires are especially problematic in rural areas. Houses and barns are often made of wood (like our house), brush fires can be common in dry periods, which provide added danger, and often there isn't any municipal water system to tap into by way of fire hydrants. All of that, along with the sheer distance that a fire truck has to travel to get to the fire in question, and you're left with little hope of saving a burning house. Our house quickly became engulfed by flames and by the time anybody got there, it was gone, burned completely to the ground. The house my father had built with his own two hands was no more.

It was an empty and devastating feeling, looking at the smoldering remains of where I had spent my childhood. I started reliving all the old feelings again. I had been so close to my mother and the home reminded me of her. To this day, whenever I walk to the mail box and look over to where my mother's house used to be, I begin to feel the pain all over again. That house was all that was left of my mother and my childhood.

Everything about it seems to produce a memory. There was a big pecan tree that stood in front of the house, and that's where we played when time permitted us to do so. I remember hiding behind that tree one time, with my hand out, asking my father for a nickel because I wanted to buy candy that my teacher was selling at school. Most of the other children were able to buy candy and pickles but I had no money and was afraid to ask my father for any. I don't ever remember him giving me any money, and that day was no different. The pecan tree still stands there today, along with our old well from which Father used to draw water to sell.

I also have fond memories of carrying wood, which we used for cooking and heating our home. I remember the boys would go about a half a mile into the woods to find an oak tree and cut it down. We would carry the wood in our arms, making as many as ten trips. This was during the winter and I can still remember how cold our hands and feet would get.

When Chris started going to school in 1983, he had to endure the same long, seventeen-and-a-half mile bus ride to Gurdon, Arkansas that I'd had to endure growing up. I would volunteer at Chris' school three days a week to keep an eye on him and to make sure he was okay. I guess I was trying to make up for what my parents never did. I wanted to make sure the teachers knew that I was interested in my child. Besides that, I missed him.

By the time Chris finished the third grade, the district law that mandated that children must attend schools in the districts in which their parents lived had changed. We transferred Chris to a much closer school in Arkadelphia.

By the time Chris had started the fourth grade I had stopped volunteering. Now I had more time for myself.

## CHAPTER TEN

# DISCOVERED BY THE CLINTONS

*If you find yourself in a fabric or craft store in the near future, take a moment to steal a really close look at a bolt or roll of any woven fabric. You might notice that it is actually composed of two sets of threads. One set of threads, the crossways, meanders over and under a stronger set of underlying threads which runs the entire length of the fabric. The direction of this set of strong underlying threads is called the grain of the fabric. Following this grain is extremely important in ensuring a well made garment. Remember the straight grain line? Make sure you stick to it, and you cannot fail. When I was ready to focus on achieving my professional and political goals, to some it appeared that I was going against the grain. As it turned out, I was diligently following my own pattern and the results were quite rewarding.*

With our son now going to school closer to our home, I felt comfortable enough to rededicate myself to the dreams I had set aside to become a full time stay at home mom.

Now it was my time. I had attended Henderson State University for two years, but discovered the university didn't offer a degree in fashion design. All my life I had dreamed of being a fashion designer; to find out that there wasn't any place in Arkansas to get a designing degree was terribly disappointing.

Undaunted, I got busy and did some research on fashion design schools. I found three of them that seemed as though they'd fit my purpose – one in Dallas, another in New York City, and a third in Little Falls, New Jersey. After some consideration, I chose the National School of Fashion Design in Little Falls and enrolled in the three-year program in 1983. This was a correspondence course which ninety-five percent of the people enrolled fail to complete. But I was so confident that I would finish that I paid all the money up front. It was hard work, but I was willing and determined. I earned my degree in two years.

I started my business, "Martha's Designs", with fifty dollars. I was a little apprehensive at first because there didn't seem to be a black business in all of Clark County with a diverse clientele. There were black barbers, black beauty shops, and black funeral homes, but they all appeared to cater to blacks only. I wanted a business that served all the people.

Stepping out on faith, I rented a small building and took in alterations to help pay the rent. At first I was afraid of not being accepted and not having enough work, but after awhile, everyone began to see how good my work was and things went well. Soon, I was able to hire a part time person and I started my designs. I designed prom dresses, wedding dresses, and all types of gowns. In no time we had more work than we could keep up with. I made enough money to pay rent, bills, and my part time employee, and I was even able to start putting money away – fifty dollars a month.

Like my father, I was determined to make my business work for me once I had started it. I knew that in order to make a profit or to at least break even I had to keep costs down and watch my spending. I started out in moderation, particularly with supplies, never purchasing more zippers, buttons, thread or other notions than I would use within a week. I saved money any way I could by doing things myself if it were possible, rather than hiring someone else to do them. When several of my fellow young entrepreneurs were ordering expensive letter-head stationery, I was satisfied with simply typing my business name on the top of plain, quality, store-bought paper.

I would go to Dallas, Texas and purchase some of the finest silk fabric they had to offer. I also found a place in California from which to order fabric and other goods. I designed and made sixteen silk dresses and took them to Little Rock to the most exclusive boutiques in the Heights, an upscale area of the city. I went to boutique after boutique, having door after door closed in my face. I remember Huie telling me that I was reaching too high, that I needed to go to some less exclusive boutiques. But I knew that it was better to sell one dress for $100 than ten dresses for $10. I knew that if I wanted to make money, I would need to go where the money was – the exclusive boutiques. "But you have to crawl before you can walk," argued Huie. "I don't want to crawl," I replied. "Nor do I want to walk. I want to *fly!*"

Despite the advice of well-meaning friends and family members who were concerned about how my ego would withstand so much rejection, I continued to haul my wares from boutique to boutique in the Heights. Finally, one day in the summer of 1986, the proprietor of Casey's Cachet, a small boutique, called me up. She wanted to buy the silk dresses I had shown her on my first sales visit and was interested in seeing more. I was so excited about the prospect of designing new dresses for Casey's that I planned a trip to New York to purchase some silk fabric. I had never flown before, and in my elation I had nearly overlooked the possibility that I might get nervous on the plane. Just so I'd feel safer and more comfortable, I bought my sister Ruth a ticket so she could come with me.

Two weeks after Casey's had selected twelve of my silk dresses, Ann McCoy, administrator of the Governor's Mansion happened to walk into the boutique and bought one of them, knowing that it would appeal to the First Lady of the state – Hillary Rodham Clinton. Mrs. Clinton loved it and decided to have the designer tracked down. She got my name, address, and phone number from the owner of Casey's and gave me a call one day, telling me how much she enjoyed my creations and promising that if her husband Bill won the 1986-1987 election for governor of Arkansas, she would wear one of my designer gowns to the Inauguration Ball. From that day forward I became interested in the political system.

Bill Clinton did, in fact, get re-elected and I traveled to Dallas to buy my fabric. I sketched out three designs and got busy making the First Lady's gown. When a woman comes to me and asks me to make a dress or a gown for her, I consider more than merely the occasion for which the garment is being made. I also take into account who the woman is and her features. I think about her age, hair color, and body frame or type. I know this is the best approach because of the smiles of satisfaction I see on my client's faces when they put on their gowns or dresses. This is the way I approached designing Mrs. Clinton's gown, too. I advised her that with her height, skin tone, hair color and body shape a dress in the color of jade green made of cracked ice on jersey would look best. Mrs. Clinton had confidence in my suggestion and was more than happy with the gown I created for her.

The night of the Inaugural Ball, Mrs. Clinton invited Huie and me to have dinner with her and Bill at the Governor's Mansion. What a wonderful gesture, I thought. Naturally I was a little nervous. Huie, on the other hand, was *very* nervous, and I had to remain calm to keep him from exploding from within. Huie's a private, reserved person, actually something of a reclusive eccentric, in fact. But he's devoted to me and supporting in everything I do, so he attended the ball with me, nerves and all. And dinner with the Clintons turned out to be very enjoyable.

At the ball, it was exciting to see Mrs. Clinton approach the stage wearing one of my original gowns. I could hardly contain my prideful smile as she passed by me. The governor wore a handkerchief in his upper pocket that I had made to match the gown. Now the gown is on display at the Old State House year round. It's a great source of pride for me to think that people from all over, touring that house, see the very dress that I designed.

Soon after that, all the boutiques that had closed their doors in my face suddenly seemed to want to do business with me. I was able to choose which ones to work with now, some located in state and some out of state. I had customers as far as Texas and a growing list of high profile clients. I received thank you notes from all over, people who were thrilled with my designs, and with how the dresses made them look. I thought back to those first days of rejection at the boutiques in the Heights. It would have been easy to become discouraged and quit. But I knew my designs were good. I knew that I had the talent necessary to succeed. And time had proven me right.

Not that I didn't have moments of doubt, of course. I'm sure everybody does. But I believe that when all is said and done, you either believe in yourself or you don't. Though you might have momentary misgivings, you can still cling to that foundation of belief. You can still wrap your arms around the idea that if you keep going, and keep having faith in yourself, and keep believing that good things will happen, by the grace of God, you'll succeed.

After the Inauguration, Huie pulled me aside and quietly told me, "Martha, you can go anywhere you want to go and I will never complain. But there are times when you're just going to have to go without me. I will never hold you back, but please don't try to pull me up with you. And our marriage will work out fine." It's an arrangement that's worked well, in fact. Since that Inauguration Ball, whenever I'm invited someplace, I always ask Huie if he wants to go. Ninety-nine percent of the time, he declines. I never push the issue, respecting instead his preference to be left alone.

In time, I came to design several dresses, skirts, and blouses for Mrs. Clinton. I traveled to the Rose law firm and Governor's Mansion several times for fittings. And the most exciting work was still ahead – when Bill became elected President, I was asked to design Mrs. Clinton's Presidential Gala gown. Now I could show off my designing skills on a national level.

I decided on the design of the gown before Mrs. Clinton left Arkansas. I created some fine sketches and Mrs. Clinton chose the one that I thought would fit her best. I had also picked the right fabric and color, red silk satin with red silk lace. I was so fortunate to have some of the town to contribute to the Gala gown. Ruth Hawthorne was instrumental in putting the gown together, and Percy Malone, Dr. H.D. Luck, Ross Whipple, George Surgeon, Raymond Toler, Bill Wright, Dan Pless, and Joyce Palla all helped defray the initial cost. The gown was beautiful. It's now on display at the Truman Library in Independence, Missouri.

*Hillary wears Presidential Gala Gown. The note on the photo says, "To Martha, The only person missing from this picture is you! Thanks for a beautiful gown." – Hillary*

My relationship with the Clintons has been nothing less than a godsend. Very simply, my business would not have been successful without their presence in my life. Oh, I sup-pose I might have found another avenue for success; I was very determined, after all. But I can't honestly say that I would have reached the same level. This is not at all to suggest that one needs a celebrity contact to succeed, or one has to count on luck or random chance. I firmly believe we make our own luck. If we work hard, and we work smart, the seemingly "lucky" breaks will happen. Doors will open to us. But even still, we never should take for granted the things and people that got us where we are. The Clintons' role in my success is something for which I will remain forever grateful.

## CHAPTER ELEVEN

# BUSINESSWOMAN

In 1987, after I had designed the Inauguration Ball gown in Arkansas, I had the opportunity to leave the state and design for J. C. Penney. Someone from their office in Dallas had called me, offering me a design position. I had no interest in leaving my family and home, however, and didn't want to put my family through the hardship of moving and settling in a new city and state. I declined the offer. Besides, I still had a yearning to do more and believed Arkansas was the place to do it.

The problem was that the upside to creating designer dresses was severely limited in Arkansas. I wasn't exactly living in New York or L.A. I needed to go off in another direction and I had plans to do just that. I had decided to begin a manufacturing business. When all was said and done, it was my only real option if I wanted to grow, as a businesswoman, and as a person.

It was another example of me deciding that crawling, walking, and even running wasn't enough. Just like those days knocking on doors in the Heights, I wanted to *fly*. And that meant spreading my wings. That meant trying something big, something different, something that could work right where I was. Designer dresses were fine, to a point. But that point had been reached, and it was time to move on.

One night, in 1987, Governor Bill Clinton invited a group of African American business owners to the Governor's Mansion to discuss how we could expand our businesses. While strolling through the governor's library, admiring all the books, the governor walked over and asked me if I'd like to have the book that I was, at that moment, holding in my hand. That was a blessing in itself, but to my further delight, he offered to sign the book for me as well. That's how I ended up with the very first autographed book in my collection: *Jelly Roll,* by Charles E. Thomas, signed by Bill Clinton. I was almost overcome with emotion, receiving that book from the governor.

During our discussion later that night about the growth of African American businesses in Arkansas, I talked to the governor about the possibilities for funding my manufacturing business. He promised he would help me, and told me that if I needed anything at all, to just call him.

Late than night, back at home, I sat down and set goals for myself. I became determined to start the manufacturing business I had mentioned to the governor. Huie, meanwhile, was dead set against the idea. "Stick with designing," he told me. Our disagreement lasted days. So at odds were we that we actually talked about separation. Ultimately, Huie came to realize that when I set my mind to something, there's really no way to change it. He decided he wouldn't stand in my way. Looking back now, Huie will tell you this decision was by far the best business decision I ever made.

Starting the business was hard. For awhile it seemed that when I would take one step forward, I would go back two. I knew that if I was going to be able to do things right, I needed a source of funding. Then I remembered what the governor said: call if I needed him. So I called, leaving a message and imagining I would probably never hear from him. Two days later, while sitting at home one afternoon, the phone rang. I picked up and found myself pleasantly surprised to hear the governor's voice on the other end. "What can I do for you," he asked. Once I got over the shock that the governor had taken the time to return a simple businesswoman's call, I explained to Mr. Clinton that I was trying to find money to expand my business, and needed some direction as to where to look. He suggested I try the Arkansas Industry Development Council. We talked a bit more and he wished me luck.

The AIDC was created to help people like me, help people with great ideas but little money to get started. They had sources of financing available, and I knew that with a loan of about $50,000, I would have everything I needed to create the kind of business that could succeed. Getting the money wasn't easy, however. It was a long and difficult process. The under-lying belief from some on the Council, though it was never explicitly said, was that a black woman could never make it in a white man's business world. The risk was too high. I would never be able to pay the money back.

It was so hard that several times during the process I just wanted to give up. But I decided to fight. If you want something you have to keep fighting and never give up. And if you don't try, you've already failed. I had fought all my life. When I was a child, whenever someone told me that I couldn't do something, I fought harder. I fought harder this time, too, and after eighteen long months, I finally secured the $50,000 loan.

It took my white neighbor, also with a manufacturing business, about three months to borrow twice as much as I had borrowed. But within a year, he had gone out of business. As far as I know, he never paid the money back. Meanwhile, I'm still in business and I paid all the money back several years ago.

After I started Dixon Manufacturing, Governor Clinton would cite me as an example as he traveled Arkansas to promote economic growth. I would use his name and influence in turn when I needed something by reminding people of the governor's commitment to developing small businesses.

CHAPTER TWELVE

# DIXON MANUFACTURING

*Dixon Manufacturing building, 1988.*

In 1988 I turned to Senator David Pryor of Arkansas to help me find some equipment for the building I had just secured for Dixon Manufacturing. I needed some sewing machines. Senator Pryor did some research and found a factory that was going out of business. One of his aides took me to see the machines there. They were old and ultimately needed a lot of work, but I was happy to be able to purchase them for a minimal cost. My plan was to use $20,000 of my loan to purchase the 5,500 square foot building I had found, then use $10,000 for repairs. The remaining $20,000 I'd use as working capital.

Plans, however, don't always go the way we anticipate. After purchasing the building I found out that there was asbestos in the tile on the floor and it could not be removed. Regrettably, I hadn't asked for an inspection of the place before moving ahead with the purchase. So I had to take the money that I planned to use for working capital and use it to cover the floor with concrete. Now I had no working capital to start production.

Regardless of how it ended up, however, my experience with Senator Pryor in helping me find equipment confirmed something to me that I had learned as a child from my mother: never be too proud to ask for help if you need it. The Senator didn't know me at all. I was a complete stranger. Yet I knew that he might be able to help me, and so I didn't hesitate to contact his office. Throughout my life, I have found that help is readily available to those who simply ask for it – humbly and sincerely, of course. Often I have seen people who are simply too proud, or perhaps too insecure to confess that they are in need of any assistance. It takes a strong person to admit to what they cannot themselves do. And yet people are often happy to lend a helping hand to an appreciative person in need.

To recoup the working capital I had lost due to the asbestos, I turned to three investors. I figured that if each one invested $5,000 in my company, that would give me the $15,000 necessary to hire employees and start production. Of the many potential investors with whom I met, I chose three people that could offer me more than money. One investor, Majeed Nahas, had managed a sewing plant in Hot Springs, Arkansas that made hospital clothes before it went out of business, and he had thirty-five years of experience managing other plants. He managed my plant until it got off the ground, which took about six months from the beginning.

Another investor was a good friend of mine, Dr. David Luck. A leader in the community, Dr. Luck had owned businesses for more than thirty-five years and knew a lot about how to maintain them. He held my hand all the way.

The third investor, Senator Percy Malone, was a good friend of mine, also, and the person who helped me the most. When I was having difficulty trying to get the loan through the Arkansas Industry Development Council, Senator Malone stepped in and put a little pressure on the Council. Although they believed I was a bad risk – a black woman trying to get into a white, male-dominated world – Senator Malone did not give up. He went to bat for me to help me eventually secure the loan.

Opening Dixon Manufacturing in 1989 helped me accomplish my dream. I now had the space to be able to make my patterns, and cut and sew them. And to all of my investors, I owe a great deal of gratitude.

Also providing me with a lot of help was Mr. William "Bill" Akins, whom I found after calling on the business department of Henderson State University. I knew that the first two years for a new business are usually the toughest and I also knew that I would need some solid business advice, particularly with keeping my spending under control. Henderson State had a small business department that helps people who are starting businesses. Bill Akins was a delightful man who took me by the hand and walked me through the feasible and non-feasible options for Dixon Manufacturing. He put a business plan together for me, something I had no idea how to put together. In fact, until that time, I didn't even know what a business plan was. The plan didn't always work out like it was written, but week after week, Mr. Akins would drop by my office to see if I needed his assistance.

I learned a lot, starting my business, and I had some things happen that made me realize how far I had come. In the process of hiring employees, for example, I was very surprised to learn that one of my white neighbors had applied for a sewing job. When I was a child and not out in the fields picking cotton, one of my jobs was cleaning this woman's mother-in-law's house. How could I have ever dreamed back then that someday that woman's daughter-in-law would be working for me?

At the beginning, I was unable to afford a marketing person. And so I set out to do the marketing myself. I got results right away. I used the publicity from designing Mrs. Clinton's 1986 Gubernatorial Inauguration Ball gown to develop a client base. Soon, we had twenty-five employees, a toll-free number, a catalog, and a website.

But, as much as my business was growing, I didn't have quite enough work to keep my employees busy all the time. And so in 1990, I began to look around the state to see what the corporate world of Arkansas could offer me. I called Tyson Foods, one of the largest meat producers in the world, and talked to Mr. Robert Cole. Mr. Cole was the buyer of smocks for Tyson, the smocks being used in the company's meat processing plants. I pleaded with Mr. Cole to give me a chance. I sent sample after sample. Finally it happened – I was given an opportunity to make some of the garments for Tyson's employees.

Eventually, I had an opportunity to meet with both Don Tyson and, later, his son John, the owners of the family company. Both of them were very willing to help me and I never expected that they would be so down to earth. In March of 1996 I was interviewed in *Southern Living*, with an accompanying photograph of me with the Presidential gala gown that I designed. Don Tyson saw the article and sent me a copy of it from Florida. That a CEO from the largest meat processing company in the world would notice me and take the time to recognize me was very gratifying.

*Martha Kid's Catalog*

I saw Don another time in Little Rock at a function where John was being honored. I walked up to him afterwards to shake his hand and say hello and I noticed he had tears in his eyes. He had been completely touched by the honoring of his son and I remember thinking how truly human the man was, and how moved I was that he showed tears in front of me. Don recently passed away, but I am still producing goods for Tyson Foods and it's a relationship I am proud to have been a part of for over twenty years.

Interestingly, it has been my experience that the higher up you go in an organization, the nicer the people. The Tysons were a good example of this. Whereas a lot of middle managers in organizations could often be cold, indifferent, or even outright hostile to a potential new vendor, the people at the top of the organizations I solicited seemed more willing to forge a good working relationship, or to at least give me a chance. Perhaps the guy at the top is moresecure with himself, no longer feeling as though he needs to prove his worth. Whatever the reason, I was always made to feel very comfortable around the Tysons. They took a chance on me, I delivered, and we began a great relationship.

In 1997, I expanded the business by adding the Martha's Kids line. We began selling school uniforms all over the country. Now I could design couture dresses and gowns, as well as uniforms for various professions and trades and schools. Soon we were providing uniforms for all the nursing schools in the state, and had an exclusive agreement to manufacture all the patient gowns for Carti Cancer Hospitals in Arkansas.

In addition to Tyson Foods, I was also proud of the fact that one of my customers – this one for the Martha's Kids line of school uniforms – was none other than Wal-Mart. I didn't have the opportunity to deal with the corporate higher-ups with Wal-Mart like I did with Tyson Foods, but I knew for a fact that Sam Walton, founder and CEO of Wal-Mart, preferred to buy American. I really appreciated that. And it didn't hurt that the Wal-Mart headquarters were located right in

Arkansas. Still, I had to deal with the Wal-Mart buyers on a state-by-state basis, as Wal-Mart had different contracts to supply school uniforms with each state for which it did so. But they were fine people to deal with – if a little slow to pay – and naturally it was quite a feather in the cap of Martha's Kids to count among its customers one of the largest companies in the world.

As with my experience with Senator Pryor, another example of me not being afraid to seek out help came with another Senator – Senator Dale Bumpers. For two years I had been trying to get my AA Certification – an affirmative action designation that would allow me access to specific government contract set-asides. Essentially the pursuit was mostly a lot of bureaucratic red tape and waiting around for responses. It was frustrating and was beginning to seem impossible.

One day Senator Bumpers was visiting Arkadelphia. I wasted little time in seeking him out, approaching him and letting him know of the difficulties I was having. He listened attentively, took my business card, and promised he'd look into it. Within mere months I received my set-aside.

Friends of mine have long marveled at my ability to approach strangers in this way. I guess, looking back at how shy I once was, I marvel a little too. And yet now it seems like such a part of me. I have found that, on balance, any given person has more in common with you than not. Going up to somebody, introducing yourself, shaking their hand, asking where they're from or what they do – it often becomes a prelude to a conversation where you find yourself surprised by your similarities, rather than disappointed by your differences. It's rare I can't find something to talk about with someone, and I always feel the better person for having made the effort. I typically learn a little something, they hopefully learn a little something, and every now and again I make myself a new friend.

As for my investors, the deal was that, when I was able to, I would buy them out. There was a kind of underlying understanding that if I didn't pay them back, that would be okay. They'd write the loss off. And, in fact, I'm pretty sure that's just what they expected would happen, though they never came out and said so. But it wasn't okay with me. I knew I'd succeed and I knew I'd be able to pay them back. With interest. In the end, after working hard, saving, and watching every penny spent, I was able to pay them all back in five short years, one of whom I gave back $10,000 for his $5,000 investment. How's that for interest?

I also paid back the Arkansas Industry Development Council its $50,000 – with interest of course. I was careful not to miss a monthly payment in order to build and protect my credit. Sometimes, I even paid twice as much per month.

There have been many gratifying things that have happened to me since I began Dixon Manufacturing. In 1995, 1996, and 1999, I was recognized as one of the "Top 100 Women of Arkansas" by *Arkansas Business Magazine.* I received congratulatory cards from around the United States, from the First Lady of Arkansas, and from the First Lady of the United States – Hillary Clinton. This was a real joy. In 2002, Dixon Manufacturing received a partner-ship award from Tyson Foods and the Arkansas Regional Minority Development Council.

*Martha Dixon, (at right) inducted into AR Black Hall Of Fame.*

It was a particular honor to be inducted into the Arkansas Black Hall of Fame in 2005. One of the best things about that night was that my siblings were in attendance and it was such a joy to see all my sisters and brothers. I actually cried, I was so happy on that night.

One of the biggest highlights of my career involved the first inauguration gown I had made for Mrs. Clinton. On February 14, 1988, I received a call from the chairman of the Tabriz Auction, one of the largest fundraisers in Arkansas. He asked me if I'd consider entering one of my gowns and I agreed. To my great delight and surprise, the gown sold for twenty-five thousand dollars.

The biggest highlight just might have been that day in July of 1997 when I was given the chance to spend a day at the White House, which allowed me the opportunity to sleep in the Lincoln Bedroom. Thrilled at this once in a lifetime chance to be so close to and personally experience an important part of American history, I excitedly shared the news with Huie and asked if he wanted to go. Yes, we had made the pact that as my career took off and took me to places that Huie might not feel so comfortable going, I would refrain from requiring him to accompany me. But this was the White House! Such a rare privilege to be invited to this most historic of our nation's buildings, and to be allowed to spend the night in one of its most prestigious rooms! I emphasized this to Huie after he declined the first time I asked. In spite of the pact, I asked again. He declined again and I decided I would not ask a third time. After all, we had agreed that the best way to preserve our marriage was for me to allow him the right to say no to opportunities like this one.

*My son, Christopher with the White House First Cat, Socks.*

I called the White House to get permission to bring my son Chris with me instead of Huie and that turned out to be a great blessing. I'd never seen Chris so happy and excited as when he played with Socks, the First Cat. Chris and I both had a blast all day. We practically had the run of the White House grounds and I had never seen such beauty. The only thing that topped the excitement of the day was ending it with a night of rest in the famous Lincoln Bedroom. Growing up in a home of modest means and having to endure backbreaking labor most of my childhood, I'd never dreamed it was possible for me to one day sleep in the White House. As great an experience as it was, and as momentous as it seemed at the time to me, it was a fitting culmination to a se-ries of momentous occasions in my life among the movers and shakers of the Arkansas political and business world over the prior years.

And all by taking a chance on a dress.

## CHAPTER THIRTEEN

# DR. MOOR

Help for me and my business came from a lot of different places, but there was one place in particular that was a seemingly-constant source of assistance.

For as long as I can remember, Dr. William Moor was known as the best doctor in Arkadelphia. He had a reputation for being firm, demanding, and somewhat of a grouchy old man. Tall and slender with piercing eyes, Dr. Moor cut a rather imposing figure to those not used to him. He became our family physician in 1967 when I got married, having been my husband's family doctor prior.

When I was going through the stressful process of securing the building for my factory, I decided I'd better talk to someone about all the pressure and disappointments that I might face, so that I wouldn't get worn down emotionally and psychologi-cally. I made an appointment to see Dr. Moor, even though I was somewhat apprehensive due to his off-putting and curmudgeon-like demeanor. I was already in a fragile state of mind and wasn't sure I could stand the additional strain of dealing with a doctor with a less than gentle bedside manner.

When I walked into his office that day he invited me to sit down across the desk from him as usual. I always thought doctors were emotionally strong and resilient people – especially Dr. Moor. But that day my eyes were opened to a surprising revelation: doctors had weaknesses, too. I was surprised to find out that Dr. Moor was depressed and, in fact, had more problems than I had, most of which revolved around his personal life which was in turmoil at the time. I sat quietly and attentively as the typically stoic Dr. Moor spoke openly to me – a mere patient – about his wife, his two children, and his grandchildren. I listened to him, even though he was on the side of the desk where the listening usually took place.

I realized that afternoon that it was a very brave and human thing for Dr. Moor to do, allowing himself to show weakness by stepping out of his comfort zone as an authority figure and just being a man, with flaws and problems like any other. From that day forward we became good friends. He would call me daily, sometimes more than once. He felt comfortable enough to talk to me, whether he had a problem or not. At twenty years my senior, Dr. Moor was like a father and mentor to me. I saw him laugh and I saw him cry. He told me things about himself that no one else ever knew.

Dr. Moor actually helped me more than he had any idea. The first time I went to the Governor's mansion to work on Mrs. Clinton's gown, he told me I had to enter through the back door. And then he laughed. It was a harmless attempt to tease and belittle me, but it had the opposite effect. It helped strengthen me. Of course I entered through the front door.

What he didn't know was that all of the Clintons' friends entered through the back door, typically picking up one of Mrs. Liza's cookies. Mrs. Liza was the head cook for the Clintons. She was an excellent one, and her cookies were delicious. One day Dr. Moor went with me to the Governor's mansion. When we left, I made sure we exited through the back door, snagging one of Mrs. Liza's cookies on the way.

When the Clintons were in the White House, Dr. Moor tried at various times, unsuccessfully, to get his resume to them, hoping for an appointment of some description. He enlisted the help of friends to deliver it, but somehow it just never made it. At least until I helped him out. The lady that Dr. Moor thought had to enter through the back door of the Governor's mansion turned out to be the only one that was able to get his resume in the door of the White House. And so the joke was on him.

There were so many other incidents like his "backdoor" joke that defined our unique friendship. He always told me he was proud of me, yet constantly found some way to put me down. What he did not know about me was the more you stepped on me the more it motivated me. He once said to me, "Have you pickinney today?" Puzzled, I looked at him and asked, "What are you saying?" Without flinching he began to repeat the question, slowly enunciating each word, "Have you picked any cotton today?" Then he looked at me and laughed. I suppose putting me down made him feel bigger. But I gave him a good blessing out that day and he never said that to me again. I suspect that Dr. Moor sometimes resented my progress, even though he claimed to be proud of me. He would often ask me what made me so strong. Maybe he was envious.

We learned from each other, though. We made observations about people, often disagreeing, but it somehow seemed to help us understand one another. One day Dr. Moor was sitting in my office having coffee, when a young black boy passed by the window with his pants hanging down to his knees. Dr. Moor made a comment about how bad the boy looked. I made the comment that white boys wore their pants the same way, to which he replied that the white boys could get away with it, since they had it made. The black boys, on the other hand, had better try a little harder. I didn't care for his answer, but after I thought about it, I turned to Dr. Moor and admitted that he was – unfortunately – right.

He gave me a valuable piece of advice one day which I have never forgotten. We were walking into a Piggly Wiggly grocery store, me with my head down, a step behind him. He turned and looked at me. "Martha!" he said, in a chiding voice. "When you walk into a place – don't matter if it's a Piggly Wiggly or Buckingham Palace – you walk in like you *own* the place!" From then on, it was always shoulders back, head up. I might not always be confident about where I'm going, but I'm sure going to look like I am. I've found people automatically treat you with more respect.

Dr. Moor was the kind of person you either disliked or loved. My family chose to love him. In the twenty years that we knew Dr. Moor, we saw him through numerous challenges and health issues, including knee and hip replacements. He seemed to get sick more often after his retirement. One night at about nine o'clock he called me to his home because he wasn't feeling well. By the time I got there he was terribly ill, vomiting frequently. I drove him to the emergency room and he was admitted immediately. I stayed with him until nearly midnight that night. That wasn't the only trip to the emergency room I had to make with Dr. Moor and eventually it got to a point where he gave me a key to wherever he was staying so that I could easily get in to check on him.

My husband and son considered Dr. Moor part of our family. He would frequently come to our home on Sundays to have dinner with us. When I would travel around the state to do measurements for nurses' uniforms, Dr. Moor would accompany me and help whenever he could. He served on the Board of Higher Education while I was serving on the State Board of Education and sometimes we would travel together to meetings and other functions that involved both groups. Later we had the opportunity to continue to be travel mates when he became chairman of the Democratic Party and I

*Dr. Moor's Note.*

was the secretary. Dr. Moor's office was next to mine and we had coffee together every single morning.

After Dr. Moor's wife died he leaned on me even more. Sometimes even a bit too much; I had a family after all. But if I tried to back away he'd send flowers or write some kind of note, telling me how much he needed my friendship. "Dear Martha," one of them began, "Each time I hear the outside door open and close, I hope it will be you...Please don't cut me out of your life." I think back sometimes to that first day I walked into his office, imagining at the time the man behind the desk being strong, detached, and seemingly unapproachable. Things, of course, aren't always what they seem. Dr. Moor's neediness was well hidden by all outward appearances. But it was met by my respect and friendship and the relationship somehow worked. His passing in 2005 left a void in the lives of me and my family. Every day we think of something he would say or something he did and we laugh. Dr. Moor is missed.

CHAPTER FOURTEEN

# POLITICS

*Have you ever been fitted for dress or a suit? Typically, even though the seamstress or tailor has already taken your measurements, they need to make sure the garment is shaping up to correctly fit you. Some form of "temporary" stitching is necessary so that you can try on the dress or suit as it is being made. The seamstress may use pins along the seams; or she may use a process called basting. Now, if there will be a lot of pressure or strain on the seam during the fittings, it is recommended that the seamstress use strong basting. I had achieved a lot of my goals by this time in my life, and was ready to expand my horizons-to "try on" or "get fitted" for some new roles, in a manner of speaking. In retrospect, I should have taken care to use some strong basting.*

Arkadelphia is a college town. It is home to two colleges – Henderson State University, with an enrollment of about 3,600 students, is a state school, and Ouachita Baptist University, about 1,500 students, is a private one. Together, both colleges are a major factor in our economic survival. Arkadelphia is where most people in Clark County do their grocery shopping, but we have very few places where you can buy clothing. The closest place is Hot Springs, which has a mall and is about forty miles from Arkadelphia. Of course Little Rock, the state capital, has malls, but at sixty-eight miles from the center of Arkadelphia, it proves a long drive to do everyday shopping for basic necessities. It is, however, your best option if you want to do some serious shopping.

Once my business got started, my home town of Arkadelphia seemed to adopt me as one of its premier citizens. Everyone was extremely nice to me. One man in particular was very special to me – Dolphus Whitten. Dolphus was a happy man and a prominent figure in the community. He would come around once a week just to give me a hug and tell me how proud he was of me. That went a long way with me. Sometimes it was just what I needed.

Three months after I started my business, I was asked by the president of the Arkadelphia Chamber of Commerce to join the organization. I agreed to join and about eight months later, I was asked to serve on the board. One day the board decided to have an advertising agency come in and take pictures, to show what the community looked like. At the next month's meeting the president had all the pictures of the community placed on display. I noticed something missing right away; there were no black people in the photographs. Clark County was twenty-one to twenty-two percent African American at the time, and yet the African American community was left out. "Where are the black folk?" I asked indignantly. "We are in the community, also." The board members made light comments, but really didn't know how to respond. The next month the display board was changed. It had black people as well as white people on it. I was grateful. "We all make mistakes" I said, "and we all sometimes live in our own little worlds and often forget to look around to see others."

When I started my business, there were three banks in Arkadelphia, none of which had blacks on their boards. I thought that as long as black people had money in the banks, they should be represented. I wrote each bank president, asking if they would consider putting a black person on their boards when they had an opening. The response that I received was incredible. Some responded in writing. Others came by my office in person, just to acknowledge that they had received my letter. Everybody was positive and willing to make changes. Now, each of the banks of Arkadelphia has at least one black person serving on its board.

One day in June of 1991, after I had written the bank letters, I was walking in the parking lot of a local Wal-Mart and met one of the community's prominent black ministers. I happened to have a copy of the letter in my car that I had sent to the banks, and asked him to read it and give me his opinion. He read it and told me the letter was good. Since his response was favorable, I asked him if he would be willing to serve on one of the boards, if asked. He answered yes, understanding that the letter was not just for me, but for all African Americans of Arkadelphia and Clark County. It was nice to reach out and make a difference. Little by little, I found myself getting more and more involved in things that went beyond my business.

DIXON MANUFACTURING, INC.
701 CLINTON
ARKADELPHIA, AR. 71923
501-246-6645

May 13, 1991

Mr. Raymond Toler, President
CITIZENS FIRST STATE BANK
506 Main Street
Arkadelphia, AR 71923

Dear Mr. Toler:

In a survey I did around the State of Arkansas, I found that Arkadelphia is more advanced in academic education and race relationships than any other town its size. That makes me proud to be a business owner here.

As the chief executive officer of one of our banks, your contribution and that of your staff are significant factors in the positive image of Arkadelphia. It concerns me, however, that no black leaders serve on any of our three bank boards. Whenever your institution prepares to replace or add a member to your Board of Directors, please take this into consideration. You could help make this "giant step" toward the continued progress of racial unity in our community. It would be nice to see!

Thanks for your time and any consideration you might give to this suggestion.

Sincerely yours,

Martha Dixon

**DMI Correspondence letter with Response letter from Merchants & Planters Bank**

CITIZENS
FIRST STATE BANK
of Arkadelphia  P. O. BOX 218 / ARKADELPHIA, ARKANSAS 71923 / (5

June 7, 1991

Martha Dixon
701 Clinton Street
Arkadelphia, Ar 71923

Dear Martha:

I want to thank you for taking the time out to write your letter of May 13, 1991 concerning minorities on the bank boards in Arkadelphia. Your letter was presented at our regular June board meeting and was noted in our minutes.

Consideration will be given in the future when replacements or additional members are added to our board.

Cordially Yours,

R.C. Toler
President

RCT/gd

**DIXON MANUFACTURING, INC.**
701 CLINTON
ARKADELPHIA, AR. 71923
501-246-5645

May 15, 1991

Mr. James Harrington
Chairman of the Board
ELK HORN BANK & TRUST
Post Office Box 248
Arkadelphia, AR 71923

Dear Mr. Harrington:

In a survey I did around the State of Arkansas, I found that Arkadelphia is more advanced in academic education and race relationships than any other town its size. That makes me proud to be a business owner here.

As the Chairman of the Board of your bank, your contribution and that of your staff are significant factors in the positive image of Arkadelphia. It concerns me, however, that no black leaders serve on any of our three bank boards. Whenever your institution prepares to replace or add a member to your Board of Directors, please take this into consideration. You could help make this "giant step" toward the continued progress of racial unity in our community. It would be nice to see!

Thanks for your time and any consideration you might give to this suggestion.

Sincerely yours,

Martha Dixon

cc: Ms. Mary Houghton
    Mr. Ron Grzywinski

---

**DMI Correspondence letter with Response letter from Elk Horn Bank & Trust Company**

---

**Southern Development Bancorporation**

605 Main Street, Suite 202
Arkadelphia, Arkansas 71923
501-246-3945
Fax 501-246-2182

June 10, 1991

Ms. Martha Dixon
Dixon Manufacturing, Inc.
701 Clinton
Arkadelphia, AR 71923

Dear Martha:

You're right.

Elk Horn Bank should have a Black director, and in fact we did have a Black director until Mahlon Martin was forced to resign his seat on the Elk Horn Bank Board when he took over as President of the Winthrop Rockefeller Foundation at the beginning of last year. We have asked the Federal Reserve Bank of St. Louis to allow Mr. Martin to continue on the Bank's Board of Directors, but so far they have not acceded to our request.

I would also note that two of Southern Development Bancorporation's Board of Directors are Black: Dr. Jackie McCray and Herman Davenport. Two other former Southern Directors Tom Shropshire and Dr. Robert Miller were also Black. Mr. Shropshire resigned due to his affiliation with the Winthrop Rockefeller Foundation and Dr. Miller, due to ill health.

Southern's management and Directors take the issue of Board membership very seriously in all the Southern companies. We believe that the Boards of the Southern companies should not only reflect their management, owners, and donors, but also the communities they serve. We are currently focusing our efforts on expanding the Board of Arkansas Enterprise Group, but I will keep in mind the need to diversify the Bank's Board of Directors as we go through that process.

Sincerely,

George P. Surgeon
President

cc: James Harrington

**DMI** DIXON MANUFACTURING, INC.
701 CLINTON
ARKADELPHIA, AR 71923
501-246-6645

May 15, 1991

Mr. Ross Whipple
Chairman of the Board
MERCHANTS & PLANTERS BANK
526 Main Street
Arkadelphia, AR 71923

Dear Mr. Whipple:

In a survey I did around the State of Arkansas, I found that Arkadelphia is more advanced in academic education and race relationships than any other town its size. That makes me proud to be a business owner here.

As the Chairman of the Board of your bank, your contribution and that of your staff are significant factors in the positive image of Arkadelphia. It concerns me, however, that no black leaders serve on any of our three bank boards. Whenever your institution prepares to replace or add a member to your Board of Directors, please take this into consideration. You could help make this "giant step" toward the continued progress of racial unity in our community. It would be nice to see!

Thanks for your time and any consideration you might give to this suggestion.

Sincerely yours,

Martha Dixon

---

**M&P Merchants & Planters Bank**
Arkadelphia, Arkansas 71923 501/246-4511    Gurdon, Arkansas 71743 501/353-6132
West Pine Office 501/246-4653

May 21, 1991

Mrs. Martha Dixon
Dixon Manufacturing, Inc.
701 Clinton Street
Arkadelphia, AR  71923

Dear Martha:

Thank you for your letter of May 15th, with reference to what the commercial banks in Arkadelphia are doing with regard to developing black leaders for future board positions.

Our Board met late last week and your letter was presented and accepted in a very positive manner. As we plan to expand our bank board's here in Arkadelphia we need to take a long look at potential black leaders and the many positive things they can bring to our respective bank's.

Again, thank you for your letter in reminding us that our bank's need better serve the entire community.

Sincerely yours,

Ross M. Whipple
Chairman

RMW/rkf

**DMI Correspondence letter with Response letter from Merchants & Planters Bank**

There were earlier examples. There was a time when the Arkadelphia Lions Club did not put out the American flag on Martin Luther King, Jr.'s birthday. Nor did other businesses, yet flags were put out for other holidays. One day, in the spring of 1988, the president of the organization, whom I had known for a long time, stopped by my office, asking if I'd like to join the organization for a fee of twenty-five dollars a year. Since I was the only black business in town, he figured it would look good if I supported the Lions Club.

I told him I would join the organization on one condition: the Lions Club would put out a flag for King Day. He responded that he hadn't considered King Day a holiday worth putting a flag out for, especially since they had only so many days on which they could put out the flag. But he promised to talk my proposition over with the other members of the organization. The very next year the flags went out on Martin Luther King, Jr.'s birthday and I paid the twenty-five dollars to join the organization. Sometimes all it takes is to ask.

My desire to want to effect change can be traced even further back. In the summer of 1968, I was working in Arkadelphia at the Levi Strauss sewing plant. For two years I sat at a machine bar ticking the pockets of men's pants. On my first day there, I noticed that there were two restrooms. One of the restrooms had two toilets and the other had ten. The black employees always used the smaller one and the white employees used the larger one. That day, I chose to use the larger one, unaware of the polite discriminatory arrangement. The black employees told me that the white people were going to beat me up because I had breached this informal agreement among the plant employees. I asked the manager if there were separate restrooms for black and white employees and he told me plainly, "No." Within three weeks, all the black employees were using the larger restroom right alongside their white counterparts. They all thanked me for reversing the ingrained assumption that the black employees weren't worthy of the larger restroom.

I suppose I am somewhat of a born people-pleaser. I have always tried to put the needs of others over my own. Growing up I tried to please my mother and I have tried to please my siblings, often doing things that they wanted me to do, even if, at times, I didn't want to do them. I believe that love tells you to set yourself aside and do whatever needs to be done.

In my adult life that philosophy has taken the form of me serving on boards that I didn't necessarily want to serve on. I have found myself going to meetings that I didn't want to attend. But I would convince myself that I needed to be there, to represent African Americans, knowing as I did that I would be the only black there. I needed to go to make a difference.

I suppose my real political work had its roots back when I had been assured that if the Clintons won the 1986-87 election, I'd be given the opportunity to design the gubernatorial gown. At that time I got busy and worked hard to make sure that I did my part in ensuring a victory for the Clintons. I started out by helping the secretary of the Democratic Party in my county. Mr. R.V. Well had become desperately ill with cancer, and I volunteered to help with the paperwork, sending out letters to all the county committee members.

When Mr. Well succumbed to the disease just eight months after being diagnosed, I asked Bill Wright, the chairman of the party, if I could take over the job. There had never been an African American in that position in Clark County. In fact, at the time, there was only one other African American on the Democratic Party committee. A fair and good person, Bill Wright gave me the job.

One of the first things I did as secretary was read the rules. I started putting things together. African Americans made up twenty to twenty-two percent of our county but had little to no representation. I learned that the county was divided into fourteen precincts and each precinct had one member that served on the quorum court. Two of the precincts were mostly African American. And so in 1987-88, I got busy and made our county Democratic Party look like our county. I worked hard to get two African American members on the quorum court. It wasn't easy. A big part of the problem was that people were just not properly informed about their rights as citizens, nor did they know much about the political process. African Americans in many districts didn't even know that they could run for the quorum court, despite the fact that they were in the majority in these districts and therefore entitled to better representation. But by 1989, I had succeeded in getting African American representation and our county was now properly represented to reflect the twenty to twenty-two percent African American population.

Emboldened by these victories, I continued to work with the county committee as secretary and eventually was confident enough in my abilities to begin working at the state level. I think I was more surprised than anyone when in 1988, I became a state committeeman.

A particularly proud moment in my political life was when I established the Democratic Party Headquarters in Clark County. I put up with a lot of opposition, but I enjoyed the challenge.

In addition to performing duties as the first African American secretary of the county, I also oversaw county elec-tions. At the end of 1988 I was asked by the governor to serve on the State Board of Elections Commission. From there, it was on to the State Democratic Executive Committee, to which I was elected in 1999.

In 2000 I was elected to serve as the Democratic National Committeewoman for Arkansas. In 2008, I was the only African American super delegate in Arkansas.

That same year, I was asked to co-chair Hillary Clinton's presidential campaign in Arkansas. I was delighted to do so. That was a very hard time for me, because I had people from both sides calling me constantly. People from in state and people from out of state would call. Whenever I went out grocery shopping people would stop me. A thirty minute trip would take me an hour and a half.

One day, while shopping in Wal-Mart, trying to avoid being stopped by people wanting to ask so many questions about the presidential race, I ran into Dr. Jansen. Mark Jansen is my personal physician, the best in the county, in my estimation. Doctor Jansen asked, "What's the hurry?" I told him about my burden as super delegate and that I was trying to dodge the inevitable questions from seemingly everybody I passed. Dr. Jansen lowered his voice and said, in as serious a tone as he could muster, "Put on a blonde wig and dark shades, and maybe you can escape." We both laughed and although I never did try Dr. Jansen's advice, I did briefly consider some kind of disguise during those days.

That same year, on Mother's Day, Hillary Clinton called me to wish me a happy Mother's Day. We talked a bit about the presidential election. She wanted to know where I stood and I told her that I would keep my promise to stand by her. Bill and Hillary had been friends of mine for twenty years, after all, and I didn't want to do anything to jeopardize our relationship. I did, however, support Barack Obama after Hillary lost the primary, doing all I could to help him in his bid for the White House.

Two years earlier, in 2006, when a new governor of Arkansas was elected, I approached the new governor with the suggestion that I select and spearhead a committee to buy our own state Democratic Party Headquarters, and maybe construct our own new Democratic Party Headquarters building. We had always leased our building and never owned it. The cost of the upkeep, which we had to pay, had become prohibitive. He said that he thought it was a wonderful idea. I was excited that the governor liked the idea, but he also told me that he would be busy with his governor duties and would have no time to help. I would be on my own.

I announced at the next state committee meeting in Hot Springs that the governor had given the okay to put in motion my plans. The plan was to buy the building that we were presently leasing. This would be a major accomplishment, because we had never owned our own building. The crowd gave me a standing ovation and many approached me afterwards to ask if they could be on the building committee.

That same year the governor selected one of his good senator friends as the new chairman of the Democratic Party. Wanting to just focus on running the party, he also didn't want to be involved with buying or building a new building. But that was fine with me. I was determined to do the job well, regardless of whatever help I would get. And so I called different people and eventually selected a seven-member committee. I chose some of the best and brightest that Arkansas had to offer. This list included a former governor, president of the Arkansas branch of the AFL-CIO, a certified public accountant, a state representative, and others. We started to work.

I personally wrote a plan, contacted the real estate agent, contacted a surveyor, got an offer and acceptance on the land and building, and contacted a bank that set up payments. After securing an architect, I wrote letters to all seventy-five counties and auxiliaries, and we developed plans for fund raising. Donations from several counties had started to come in. Everything was going well.

Then one day the chairman of the Democratic Party called and asked to see me. Before I left home for the meeting, Huie shared his prediction of what the meeting would be about. "The chairman wants to take control of your project," Huie remarked, "since it's going so well. He wants to take the credit."

I found out once I got to the meeting that Huie had guessed correctly. The chairman started by telling me how well I was doing and then adamantly insisted that if we worked together, it could be even better. But I recognized male chauvinism when I saw it. The chairman wanted control. Pure and simple. I knew he had no intention of working with me. And I also knew that, being chairman, he could take the project if he wanted it. Soon, the pretenses were dropped and the chairman warned outright that he could stop the flow of money for the building if I didn't cede control. With no choice, I watched the chairman take over my project. But I remained loyal to the party notwithstanding.

The problem was, as a previous state senator, the chairman had never been connected to the Arkansas Democratic Party and didn't know how it was run. Both he and the governor were new to the party at the state level, and neither one could lead the party or tell the other how it was done. As time went on, there were many mishaps, and important tasks were left undone. My help was rebuffed. The chairman's position was that he was the chairman, and if he didn't know what to do about something, he didn't want to be told. He would simply figure it out for himself and do it his way, right or wrong.

In 2008, I ran for re-election as the National Committee-woman. True to form, the chairman didn't understand the rules on how the election was to be held, and I made the mistake of telling him. As always, he insisted on doing things his way. I even talked to the Democratic National Committee to make certain I was right. In the end, the election was held correctly, the way that I knew it needed to be held. But from that point on, I was definitely confirmed as being on the chairman's "Do Not Like" list.

The classification is actually a bit too mild to describe his feelings towards me. On the evening of June 19, 2008, at about 8:30, I received a call from the chairman. It was beyond unfriendly. He told me he was going to do all he could to make sure I was not re-elected, and assured me that he had the necessary help to do just that. This was the night before the Southern Regional meeting in Mobile, Alabama. It is at this meeting that important connections are usually made and/or confirmed.

Needless to say I didn't sleep very well that night, thinking about the phone conversation with the chairman. I tried to catch what little sleep I could, though. But at 3:00 a.m., I had to rise to get around and catch my flight to Mobile. I was nervous and rattled by the threat from the chairman to effectively end my political career. But beyond losing a few hours sleep, I vowed not to let his posturing bother me. I intended to stand up to his political bullying and keep fighting, no matter what obstacle he threw in my path.

I hadn't fully realized, however, that my previous battles with the chairman had already taken a toll on me. Standing with some committee members outside on the sidewalk the next day in Mobile, I fainted, hitting my head on the ground and cutting my face. The whole time that I was being helped up and attended to, all I could think about was what the chairman had said to me. One of the committee members called the paramedics and they took my vital signs. They wanted to take me to the hospital, but I refused. I didn't want Huie finding out. Finally a couple of the committee members assisted me to my room and the next morning I was fine. I returned to the meetings the following day.

The experience, however, forced me to take an accounting of my heavy involvement in the party. I began to think that it might be time to slow down or even quit altogether. No matter what, it was clear that I had to at least release some of the stress the involvement was causing. My face was sore for about four months after the incident and the scar was visible for over a year. Whenever I had to make an appearance, I put makeup on to cover it.

I finally decided I wanted to get out of the race, but some of my friends convinced me to stay in. I continued, but my lack of desire led to a lack of real effort on my part, and in the end I lost the election.

It must be said, though, that the loss ended up, surprisingly, being one of the best things that could have happened to me. I hadn't realized that the Democratic Party had consumed me, heart and soul. Since the loss and my decreased participation in party politics, Huie often says that he has found his wife again. Not having to always tend to party business has also given me time for other pursuits, such as writing about my life. I now thank God for that election loss because it has helped me to regain focus on other important things in life.

Reflecting on the more recent 2010 election, I truly know that I am blessed. I got out just in time. I have never seen anything like this election. There was a time when elected officials did not openly support candidates during elections. If you held office or any position within the Democratic Party, you were discreet about any assistance you provided for candidates. The 2010 election has completely changed every-thing. The entire political system is broken and I can't help but ask, where are the ethics?

The Democratic Party is not sticking together. It seems like all across America no one wants to say President Obama's name or talk about the good things that our president has done. It's as if the Democrats have fallen asleep and none are slumbering more deeply than those in Arkansas. I thought that after the election was over in Arkansas our chairman would come out and acknowledge our loss, but at the same time commit to regrouping and doing better. I happen to believe our current governor is one of the best that Arkansas has ever had. He's doing an excellent job and I hope he will continue his fine work and extend it into efforts to improve the Democratic Party, which needs a serious overhaul. It seems as though we Democrats have let the Republicans lead while we shamefully follow.

When President Obama took office in January 2009, every-one wanted to ride his coat tails. Now, after fewer than two years in the White House, Obama is suddenly like poison ivy. Our Democrats are afraid to speak his name. This reminds me of a situation that occurred with another one of the "best" governors that Arkansas ever had. In 1996 our Democratic Party did not stand behind him. Increasingly it seems like our political and business leaders – those whose job it is to imple-ment policy and drive the economy – are out for themselves, little concerned about the good of the country. And many of us remain uninformed, allowing the alarming trend to continue.

The question is: where do we go now?

The relationships between people are like thread: one can't pull left while another pulls right and expect the bond to withstand such pressure. It will surely break from the strain. The Democratic Party is like a family, with threads of shared goals and ideals. If one gets weak, the material will tear. The party is only as strong as the common threads running through it. Currently, our threads are breaking and tearing.

On a larger scale, the human race is like a patchwork quilt, with pieces of varying designs, shapes, and colors stitched together to make a whole. Each of us has a part to play and adds our own special element to the hodge-podge family of humanity.

A lifetime of putting together garments – from designing, to measuring, cutting, and sewing – has obviously inspired my worldview. You don't have to have a doctoral degree to under-stand the problems of our perilous world; we all want the first piece of pie. In a way, what is happening in the political and economic landscapes in the United States right now is little more than a misunderstanding, a misunderstanding among Americans from Wall Street to Main Street. What's misunderstood is that each of us is uniquely able and obligated to impact the larger social, political, and economic picture. We have to first realize that though we differ, we are in this together for the good of the entire nation and ultimately the world. The climate that encouraged selfishness and greed is no longer viable for us if we hope to turn around the economic plight we are in now. Once we understand this, we must let our elected officials know that we will not tolerate selfishness and greed in the state capitals or Washington, nor in the boardrooms and meeting halls.

With the Democratic Party pulling one way and the Republican Party pulling the opposite, it will be doubly challenging to survive these difficult economic times. The now tenuous common threads that bind us as Americans will surely break if we don't do some serious mending. We need to double stitch and tie the knot not once but maybe three times so the thread won't slip through. If we don't watch ourselves we will come unraveled.

We often tell our children to stop and reassess their lives and get on the right track. As leaders of our generation, we need to follow our own advice. It will take a lot of hard work, but it can be done. We all have a part to play. Let us start with ourselves.

## CHAPTER FIFTEEN

# REGROUPING

On a Sunday morning, the fifth of February, 2006, I was in church when a friend took me aside, having just received a phone call with urgent news for me: my company building was on fire. I hurried over in time to watch the fire department trying desperately to save it, calling Huie on my cell phone on the way. The fire department was losing the battle. Huie arrived shortly thereafter and stayed as the building burned to the ground. For my part, I had to leave. It was more than I could bear to watch my business being reduced to ash and rubble.

The building was a total loss and I felt as though I had lost a child. For twenty years, my business had operated out of that building. I had started it with next to nothing, nurtured it, gave it everything I had, watched it grow and prosper. I guided it through good times and bad. And it had repaid me in more than monetary terms. I grew right along with it. And now it was gone.

I couldn't help but think back to the house I had grown up in, also burned to the ground, and how I had felt a piece of me had been lost with it. The building fire was strikingly familiar with its sense of unrecoverable loss and the feeling of emptiness that comes along with it. I cried for days.

*Courtesy of Daily Shiftings Herald.*

I also found myself thinking about the strange coincidence of bad events that seemed to befall me in the cold month of February. Sometimes I think that month is haunted. Certain dates in particular. My mother gave birth to me and my twin at the age of thirty-six. My twin died February 1, 1948, buried on February 5. My mother passed away February 1, 1982, buried February 5. Mother died when I was thirty-six, her age when I was born. She was seventy-two at the time of her death. Thirty-six years after her death, I will have my seventy-second birthday.

After I was all cried out from the loss of my business, I prayed and thought about what to do. Word had gotten out and people were calling to see if they could help. Even Bill and Hillary Clinton called. I was touched by all the support and I knew that, if I wanted to, I could rebuild. With the insurance proceeds and the offers of help, I might be able to build an even more successful business.

The challenge was attractive. I thought long and hard about it. I missed the business dearly. It had become a part of me, and it was appealing to think I could get it back and things could be like they were once again, with the hustle and bustle and energy of a building full of machinery and busy employees. It's excit-ing, after all, and I had missed the adrenaline. I began to realize how much I actually fed off of the energy of the company.

Ultimately, however, I decided that twenty years was enough. I had to be realistic. I knew it would be more than a year before I could have a new building, full of equipment, up and running. And by then I would have lost all of my employees and would have spent months trying to replace them with equally-skilled workers. Plus, I wasn't exactly getting any younger. I was reaching an age where I was beginning to look forward to retirement, not to taking on the enormous challenge of running a successful enterprise. No, after much prayer and deliberation, I decided it was best to call it quits.

It was quite an adjustment, not getting up early every morning to be at the plant by 7:00 a.m. It took about a year before I fully got my bearings. But I wasn't completely out of the business. I think it would have been impossible for me to have just quit cold turkey, and so I kept a piece of the company and kept it running.

There were actually three elements to my company. Martha's Kids sold private and public uniforms, mainly to schools. That branch of the business had an extensive customer base and an even better reputation. That was worth more than the building or the equipment, and I was able to sell it off at a handsome profit. That enabled me to take another portion of the business and give it away. I knew that there was no real black business operating out of Arkadelphia that catered to everybody – blacks and whites alike. Mine had been the only one, and I hated to think of the town without one decent-sized, black-owned enterprise. And so I gave the nursing uniform part of the business to a former employee, a black woman who understood the business and who I thought could make a go of it. Unfortunately, after a mere six months, to my disappointment, the nursing uniform business had gone bankrupt.

Meanwhile, I hung on to the part of the company that produced uniforms for the food processing industry – keeping my relationship with my one major customer, Tyson Foods. I still had some great contacts there, including Mike Roetzel, Vice President of Purchasing who had been of so much help to me, navigating me through the intricacies of dealing with such a large company. I ran the business out of an office I set up in my home, and began working with another company to fulfill the Tyson orders. It worked well, and still does to this day, and although I will never reach the level of business I had when all three branches of my company were going full-force, it's enough to keep me motivated and busy.

CHAPTER SIXTEEN

# FRIENDS AND REFLECTIONS

If you live long enough, God sees fit to bless you with a whole circle of friends. Joyce Palla is one. I got to know Joyce In 1989 right after I started my business and she'd often travel around the state with me. Joyce is the kind of friend who tells it like it is, not necessarily what you want to hear.

Karla Bradley is also a friend. Karla and I got to know each other as we worked in the Democratic Party. We would go to the national meeting and room together. We'd stay up at night talking about politics and got to be good friends.

Another good friend is my cousin, Annie Abrams, my confidant. I can always call on her if I need someone to talk to.

And every Friday at the Rotary Club I sit at the table with a group of friends whose company I very much enjoy. There are people in the club it would have at one time been impossible to imagine me being social with. One of them is a man from my youth. In 1965, just starting college, I went to work in private homes, ironing to make money for my education. I had been working for one family for about two months when their son spit on me. I told his parents but his parents said and did nothing. I quit that very day and never went back. Now, some forty years later, that boy and I are both members of the same Rotary Club. He doesn't remember that I was the young lady that worked for them, and that he once spit on me.

If I wanted to expend the energy, I suppose I could remain bitter about a lot of things that happened to me growing up. But I decided a long time ago that bitterness holds you back. It's my mother's influence, with her quiet strength and loving spirit, that allows me to be able to forgive people who have wronged me. Mother taught me in word and deed that to forgive is godly and to hold on to bitterness only hurts you and stops you from growing.

Sometimes friends come back from out of the past. I was so surprised when Annie Lockhart, one of my classmates from Henry Bell High school, called to tell me that another one of our classmates, Laura Neal, was home for about ten days. Annie said that there were still about ten or eleven of our classmates living in Arkansas, all retired now. Wouldn't it be a good idea if we could all get together and have a little reunion? she suggested. We decided to hold it in my home and I found myself very surprised when we all met. There were six girls and three boys. Laura came, always a special friend of mine. Shirley Gulley was a good friend of mine, too, when we were in school, but somehow we had lost touch with each other. It was good seeing her as well.

Emma Cooks and Mary Walker were there, too. I usually run into them two or three times a year around town. I see Annie Lockhart the most, bumping into her while I'm out shopping here and there. I sometimes see Charles Hatley and his wife while shopping at Wal-Mart. C.L. Allen and James Edwards I almost never see, maybe five times total since high school. And so it was a wonderful gathering. We all reminisced and had a good time. We called one of our classmates from Wisconsin, Harry Todd, and put him on a speaker phone, each of us saying hello to him. We all agreed to do it again, trying to get even more of our classmates the next time. The thing that touched me the most was when they all said how proud they were of me. It was a wonderful thing to hear and it brought tears to my eyes.

My life has been more than I ever expected. Life is like a garment that goes on and on, with different sections that must be intricately woven and connected to other parts. The garment of life is immeasurable; thus I cannot measure my life. I am sure of one thing. If God should take me home at this moment, I can say that I have gotten more than my share out of life. I cannot complain.

Out of all that I have been through in my life, I have always received the biggest thrill from trying to climb the ladder. There's a burst of energy with each step. And I have found that it's not always a bad thing to be the underdog. When you're at the bottom, you can always go up. If, on the other hand, you're already on top, there's no place to go but down.

I have found that there is something within me that keeps driving me, and somehow it won't let me give up. I believe that if there's a goal you want to reach and you want it bad enough, you mustn't give up. Regroup and keep trying. You will reach your goal. I suppose my father taught me that. I have always had the same level of ambition as my father.

It makes me wonder at people who don't have the drive, who don't have any passion. It may be true that not everyone is meant to be an entrepreneur and run his or her own business, but everyone does have some calling or purpose in life to fulfill. There is so much good out there that a person can do or be a part of. A friend once told me that God gave us all a mind and he expects us to use it, hopefully in a good way. I think we all were placed on this earth for some reason, and those reasons are as varied and as different as we are.

The fact is, everybody can be creative in what they do. I b elieve that we must find the creative part of us within. Everybody has such a part and it is this that will point us towards our purpose. For me, I knew early on that it was being an entrepreneur and a dressmaker. I knew it when I was eight years old. I knew it when I spent those long days in the hot sun picking cotton. There had to be more for me. There had to be a higher calling, a bigger reason to live. But who could ever have imagined that there I'd be, using cotton – the same stuff I had picked as a child – to make beautiful creations, making some-thing of beauty out of that which had once represented such ugliness to me? Who could have known that, someday, I'd be making something out of nothing?

And yet, this is what we each can do. We can create value where there was no value before. We can make something worthwhile, where there was nothing of worth before. And more importantly – by so doing – we can make ourselves valuable, make ourselves worthwhile. When we create some-thing, we help create ourselves. We become transformed. When we find – and follow – our purpose, we are truly alive.

Find your purpose. Step back and take a hard look at where you are today. What are your circumstances? How can you make your life better? What are your strengths and talents? How can you use them to succeed and excel?

A person has to very simply take control of his or her own life. You have to learn as much as you can about any situation you're in. Earlier I mentioned my attitude towards my own health issues – how I keep myself informed and ask my doctor every question I can think of so as to better understand what's going on with my body. It's empowering, and it's an attitude I carry with me about everything in life. Nobody else will look after you and your interests as well as you will. No matter what doctor or lawyer or accountant or business manager you have in your corner – no matter how talented and wise they are – you have to understand where you are and what you need to do on any given issue. People can give advice, but you need to know how that advice is going to help you, and even if there are other options available that you know will be better for *you* specifi-cally. In the end analysis, only *you* know what's right for you.

When I was a child, it seemed impossible that I could extricate myself from the poverty that was weighing me down. My options were limited, and yet I was able to rise above it all. I look at the options kids have today and I marvel. We live in an age where anything can happen and possibilities are limitless. There are more resources and choices available to us than ever before. If you're a young person and you're lamenting your perceived lack of opportunities, you need to look a little harder. If you want to do something, you can find a way to do it. Find a need and fill it. Always remember that somewhere, there's a person that needs what you have, a means by which you can take your talent, hidden though it may be, and let it shine.

I find myself grateful for my humble beginnings. Perhaps it was the poverty that stoked my desire. Perhaps it is the relative ease and comfort of today's luxury that is, in some ironic way, the guilty culprit in the complacency of some of today's youth. And yet, there is always something to strive for, some way to make one's life better and, by so doing, make one's world a better place. There is always something worth struggling for.

This struggle is a part of life. It's the adversity that will make you strong. I drew strength from being put down. I became motivated by my circumstances and by the people who told me I couldn't achieve something. My goals were always high. I was told time and again to start lower. "You'll have less of a fall," people would say. But I never planned on falling. And it seemed to me that whether you fall from a low place or a high place, you're still going to end up on the same ground. Might as well start high.

You will reach moments when you will want to throw up your hands and quit. These are the moments you will need to be at your strongest. There is a light at the end of the tunnel. You have to keep going.

And once you're there, you must keep going still. I believe there should be no stopping point in a person's life. Each day when you get up you should do something constructive. Each night make a plan for the next day. You might not get through everything on your list, but put whatever remains on a schedule for the next day and keep going. Sometimes you might plan a "do nothing" day, and that's all right, too. We all deserve one of them. But there's a big world out there, full of possibilities and opportunities, and it is likely you have not yet done your part.

Quite often, I'm asked what the secret to business success is. Many times young entrepreneurs will come to me and seek advice, looking for the key. For me, it was always staying on top of things. I knew how to delegate, but I never lost track of who was ultimately responsible for the company's successes and failures. Too often I see business owners who think their company can run itself. This sounds like a rookie mistake, but I see it most often from business owners who have already enjoyed some success. They reach a certain level, congratulate themselves on a job well done, and then just assume that their company will remain at that level, or even grow beyond it.

The reality is, if you begin to take your business, and customers, for granted, you'll slowly but surely start to see your business decline. Sometimes it's so slow that you don't even realize it. You just imagine that the people you've put in charge will keep things going. But without your close involvement, that doesn't always happen. Nobody, after all, has more of a stake in your business than you. Nobody will ever care as much about it as you do. You might think the people to whom you've delegated the most responsibility feel the same attachment to the company as you feel. But they don't and it's just not reasonable to expect that they would.

This doesn't necessarily mean that you have to spend twenty-four hours a day, seven days a week, in the office. Life is a balancing act. I love my work, but even in the best of times, there's still a reason they call it "work". You need to take some time for yourself and for your family. You have to remember the other priorities in your life. I enjoyed making money, but for me it was never about the money. It was about the creative process. The money came as a natural result of that process; my interest in the money was more along the lines of what I could do with it.

I like to think I used it well. I've taken cruises, traveled to South Africa, Europe, Taiwan, the Holy Land, and all kinds of other places that I wouldn't have even dared dream of as a child, picking cotton.

But of course, I always keep something else in mind, as well: I would not have been successful without all of the shoulders that I stood on for so many years; all the love and teachings of my parents and siblings; and the love of my husband and son. I have been truly blessed. God has seen fit to bestow much upon me. There's no doubt in my mind that my strength, my confidence, my desire to succeed, and indeed the very talent that assured it, came Heaven sent. But all of us have gifts of this nature. We need merely to look within, to pray for direction, and to remain still and listen to what the universe is trying to tell us. There is a path for us all. I found mine.

I have also learned that the path does not end. As we grow and reach different points in our lives, our paths shift. We are constantly presented with new challenges and new opportunities. Life is an amazing journey, a journey of constant discovery. I remain awed by what each day brings me. Each day is a welcome and exciting sight to behold. One never knows what's coming next. It has been a wonderful ride for me so far. And now? I'm just waiting to see what God has in store for me next.

- End -

APPENDIX

# CORRESPONDENCES, NOTES & NEWSPAPER CLIPPINGS

**Governor's Mansion**
LITTLE ROCK, ARKANSAS
October 6, 1986

Ms. Martha Dixon
208 S. Seventh
Arkadelphia, AR 71973

Dear Ms. Dixon:

    I wanted to let you know how much I am enjoying the dress you made that I bought from Casey's here in Little Rock. I have received so many compliments on it and it is due largely to your talent in designing and making it. I would be happy to publicize the fact that I am wearing a dress that you made whenever I have the opportunity to do so. One other idea I would like to share with you is that if all goes as well as I am hoping and the Governor is re-elected in November, I would like to discuss with you your designing one of my outfits for the inaugural activities. I would particularly like to discuss your designing the dress I would wear to the inaugural ball or similar dressy event that we might hold. If this idea interests you, please contact me after the election so we may discuss it further.

    In the meantime, I hope your business continues to grow and that you reap the success you obviously deserve. With best regards, I am,

                            Sincerely yours,

                            HILLARY RODHAM CLINTON

HRC:sjm

    cc: Mr. Percy Malone

The Smithsonian Institution gratefully acknowledges
the generosity of the Samsonite Corporation
on the occasion of
the donation of Hillary Rodham Clinton's Inaugural gown
to the First Ladies Collection
at the National Museum of American History.

---

The Secretary of the Smithsonian Institution
and
The Director of the
National Museum of American History
request the pleasure of the company of

Ms. Martha Dixon

at the presentation of
the Inaugural gown of Hillary Rodham Clinton

on Monday morning, the sixth of March
at ten o'clock

The Ceremonial Court
National Museum of American History
Mall entrance on Madison Drive, Northwest
Washington, District of Columbia

R.s.v.p. to the
Office of Special Events
202 357-3306

with us.

Best,
Hillary

---

Dear Martha,
 Thanks for your note. I have really enjoyed getting to know you. I hope you're swamped with business! Stay in touch

Your family will have a Happy and Prosperous New Year.

Best regards,
Hillary

1-17-87

Dear Martha,

Thank you for helping to make this Inauguration the best ever. I loved wearing your creation and, just as much, getting to know you. Please stay in touch with me. I trust you and

THE WHITE HOUSE
WASHINGTON

March 3, 1995

Martha Dixon
Route 1, Box 500
Arkadelphia, Arkansas  71923

Dear Martha:

I saw the recent <u>Arkansas Business</u> list, "Top 100 Women in Arkansas," and thought it was a fine recognition of your many achievements.

You have a great deal to be proud of, and I wanted to offer my congratulations.

Sincerely,

Bill    Good for you

*Hillary*

THE WHITE HOUSE
WASHINGTON

May 8, 1996

Martha Dixon
President
Dixon Manufacturing, Inc.
701 Clinton Street
Arkadelphia, Arkansas 71923

Dear Martha:

Congratulations on being selected by <u>Arkansas Business</u> as one of the *Top 100 Women in Arkansas* for 1996. You should be proud of this well-<u>deserved</u> recognition of your achievements and your contributions in Arkansas.

Hillary and I applaud your accomplishments and wish you the best in your future endeavors.

Sincerely,

Bill

(Miss seeing you - Hope you're well

THE WHITE HOUSE

April 15, 1997

Martha Dixon
701 Clinton Street
Arkadelphia, Arkansas 71923

Dear Martha:

    Thank you for sharing with us your new Martha's Kids school apparel catalogue. You make a very appealing presentation of your merchandise with those delightful Perritt School models! I wish you the very best in this new business endeavor.

    With warmest personal regards, I remain

               Sincerely yours,

               Hillary Rodham Clinton

DIXON MANUFACTURING, INC.
701 CLINTON
ARKADELPHIA, AR. 71923
501-246-6645

May 13, 1991

Dr. Bob Fisher, President
Clark County Industrial Council
518 Clay Street
Arkadelphia, AR 71923

Dear Dr. Fisher:

When I spoke to you sometime ago, you indicated that bylaws do not rule out the expansion of the Clark County Industrial Council Executive Board. As I looked through the very nice, new CCIC brochure, I regretted not seeing a single female face.

A recent speaking engagement for the National Women's Business Council reminded me of the importance of women in the business world. The Clark County Industrial Council could make an important statement to prospective industries regarding the progressive climate of our community by the addition of a woman to their Executive Board.

Please consider this as a serious and viable suggestion for progress.

Sincerely yours,

Martha Dixon, Owner

cc: Mr. Jim Dane, Executive Director
    Clark County Industrial Council

P.S. I *do* think a woman's presence would be a real asset to your board ... if not me, then someone else!

M.D.

**STATE OF ARKANSAS**
BILL CLINTON
GOVERNOR

January 11, 1988

Martha Dixon
Route 1
Arkadelphia, AR 71923

Dear Martha:

Hillary and I would like to thank you for the kindness shown us with the robes. They are great!

We truly appreciate your friendship and your thoughtfulness for remembering us during this special season.

We hope you are blessed this holiday season with good friends and much happiness!

Sincerely,

Bill Clinton

Office of the Governor • State Capitol • Little Rock, Arkansas 72201 • 501-371-2345

February 9, 2006

Martha and Huie Dixon
1155 Helmes Road
Arkadelphia, Arkansas 71923

Dear Martha and Huie:

    I was very sorry to learn about the fire, but so grateful for your safety. Know that you are in my thoughts and prayers, and if I may be helpful in any way, please let me know.

    With blessings and positive thoughts, I remain

        Sincerely yours,

        Hillary
        Hillary Rodham Clinton

**WILLIAM J. CLINTON**
4/2/56

Dear Martha —

Hillary and I were heartsick about your fire — I hope you had insurance. Regardless, knowing you, I know you'll get up and go on — let me know if I can help —

Best,
Bill

---

THE WHITE HOUSE
WASHINGTON

January 28, 1999

Martha Dixon
701 Clinton Street
Arkadelphia, Arkansas 71923

Dear Martha:

Happy Birthday! Hillary and I want to wish you the very best on this special occasion and a happy, healthy year to come.

Sincerely,

Bill Clinton

# HILLARY RODHAM CLINTON

December 21, 2007

Martha Dixon
1155 Helms Road
Arkadelphia, AR 71923

Dear Martha:

    I cannot thank you enough for participating in "The Hillary I Know" video. I count many blessings, but especially the friendships I have enjoyed, and the opportunities I have had to make a difference in the lives of others. They have made all the difference in my life, too.

    I will be ever grateful for the faith you have vested in me to lead our country as President and hope the holidays and the coming New Year bring you joy and nothing but good things. I look forward to seeing you again soon.

    With gratitude for your friendship and best wishes for the holiday season, I am

Sincerely yours,

*Hillary*

Hillary Rodham Clinton

*Thanks so much*

4420 NORTH FAIRFAX DRIVE, ARLINGTON, VA 22203-1611    TEL (703) 469-2008    FAX (703) 962-8600
www.HillaryClinton.com
*Contributions to Hillary Clinton for President Exploratory Committee are not deductible for federal income tax purposes.*
Paid for by: Hillary Clinton for President Exploratory Committee.

# HILLARY RODHAM CLINTON

August 8, 2008

Martha Dixon
1155 Helms Road
Arkadelphia, AR 71923

Dear Martha:

    Thank you for the difference you made in our campaign. I want to personally acknowledge the important role you played as a Co-Chair of my Arkansas campaign. I am so grateful for everything you did to contribute to our exciting victory in Arkansas.

    We should always be proud of what we accomplished together. Our campaign broke barriers and records, and through it all, through all the highs and lows, you, and millions of women across the country, stood by me. We have kept faith with the women and men who came before us. They held fast to the vision that one day a woman might hold the highest office in our country. Wherever I traveled, I saw mothers and fathers whispering to their children, "See, you can be anything you want to be." From now on it will be unremarkable to think that a woman can be President of the United States – and that is truly remarkable!

    As you know, our work is never done. There is so much to do to keep our families safe and healthy, and to ensure that all children live up to their God-given potential. We must work vigorously to unite our party and win back the White House in November. And we must never abandon our shared vision for what our country can achieve.

    With gratitude for your friendship and warm regards, I am

                    Sincerely yours,

                    Hillary Rodham Clinton

*Thanks so much*

4420 NORTH FAIRFAX DRIVE, ARLINGTON, VA 22203-1611   TEL (703) 469-2008   FAX (703) 962-8600
www.HillaryClinton.com
*Contributions to Hillary Clinton for President Exploratory Committee are not deductible for federal income tax purposes.*

Paid for by Hillary Clinton for President Exploratory Committee.

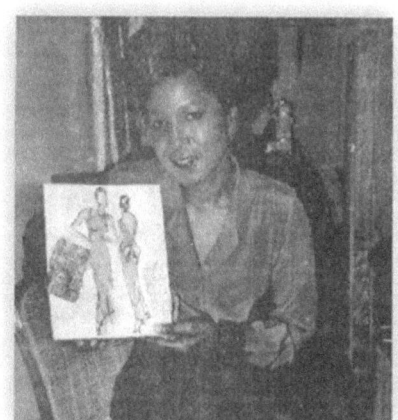

*Sketch of Gown for the Tabriz Auction.*

*Martha Dixon in her shop.*

# Hillary wears gown of local designer tonight

**By LOUISE BUCKELEW**

Viewers watching the inaugural events on television this evening will probably get a glimpse of Hillary Clinton wearing a gown designed and created in Arkadelphia by Arkadelphians.

**Martha Dixon is gown's designer.**

Martha Dixon, owner and creative designer of Martha's Designs located at 701 Clinton Street, designed and manufactured the garment which Mrs. Clinton is expected to be wearing for this evening's inaugural festivities.

The fitted bodice of the elegant red gown is constructed of French re-embroidered ribbon lace. It is embellished with hundreds of hand-sewn crystals, and lined with silk face satin.

The simplicity of the jewel neckline and long, fitted sleeves add to the understated elegance of the garment. The waistline is dropped in front and bordered with matching lace scallops.

The floor-length skirt is self-lined and constructed of matching four-ply silk crepe. The fitted skirt is accented with a series of six pleats on the back, and flows with an abbreviated train.

This is the second gown Martha has created for Hillary in conjunction with inaugural ceremonies. Hillary's gown for the 1984 Governor's Inaugural Ball was also designed and created by Mrs. Dixon.

Martha contacted Hillary immediately after the election, hoping to submit gown designs for consideration. Ann McCoy, long-time Clinton staff member in Little Rock, contacted Martha in mid-December, requesting that she come to Little Rock to discuss sketches of proposed gowns.

The final selection was the design that Martha suggested would look best on Hillary. The only change from the original sketch was the sleeve length.

After receiving the "go-ahead," a muslin version of the gown was made and fitted on a return trip.

Martha then flew to Dallas to select fabrics from the renowned Richard Brooks Fabrics. She stayed in Dallas three days, consulting with Richard Brooks, and completing the preliminary construction of the garment.

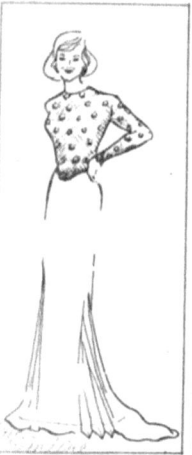

With the assistance of Ruth Hawthorne and three additional trips to Little Rock for fittings and *Please see GOWN, page 2*

*Courtesy of Daily Shiftings Herald.*

*Huie and Martha at the
The Arkansas Black Hall of Fame Gala.*

**Portfolio** By Rosalyn Story

# Martha Dixon
## *Designer and Entrepreneur*

**Dressmaker**

It seems like ages ago that the inaugural party train powered through Washington, transforming the button-down, dressed-for-success town into a sequined city trimmed with touches of Arkansas chic.

The First Lady, who is as well known for not obsessing over her wardrobe as Nancy Reagan was for flaunting hers, met the fashion challenge during inaugural week, owing some of her new-found elegance to a new name in the world of design—Martha Dixon.

To be sure, Martha Dixon is not an haute couture insider, nor is her name bandied in the company of the Ralph Laurens, the Donna Karans, and the Adrienne Vittadinis. Her design studio, in Arkadelphia, Ark., is a considerable distance from Paris, Milan and Seventh Avenue. But when Hillary Rodham Clinton sported a red crepe French-embroidered gown at a televised gala during inauguration week she focused a national spotlight on the talents of a woman who, in eight years, rose from an unemployed Arkansas housewife who had yet to sell her first dress, to a favorite designer of the president's wife.

It is an American success story true to the grass-roots tradition of Bill Clinton himself and adds support to a new myth—that in Arkansas, all things are possible. In 1986, Dixon, at 40, was a mother of an 11-year-old child, with a design degree from a correspondence course and a husband laid off from a well-paying job at Arkadelphia's Reynolds Aluminum plant. Though she had opted to stay at home and rear her son, she was no stranger to labor. Growing up in Arkadelphia's indigent black community, she was the 17th child of 20 born to a minister/truck patch farmer and his wife.

The desire to sew was born of an early inspiration. Dixon, who remembers wearing clothing fashioned from flour sacks, envied a young schoolmate who owned a sweater, and vowed to make one for herself on her mother's machine. Later, after high school, Dixon earned tuition money for Henderson State University in Arkadelphia by working as a domestic. However, the school did not offer a degree in design, and Dixon opted out of college in favor of a three-year correspondence course she'd seen advertised in a magazine. Dixon finished the Little Falls, New Jersey Commercial Technical Institute design course in one year, with straight As.

In the early '80s, Dixon dusted off her sewing skills and went to work doing alter-

*Hillary Clinton shines in a Martha's Design original.*

ations in the back of a dry cleaner's shop that she also managed. In her spare time, she designed and stitched a few garments and carried them to boutiques in Arkadelphia and nearby Little Rock, only to have more than a few doors closed in her face. "I am not shy," says Dixon. "I believe if you want something, ask for it."

Dixon persisted and eventually convinced some shop owners to carry Martha's Designs—fitted, high-fashion apparel in classic conservative style. Hillary Clinton discovered Dixon's work when her assistant, on the lookout for clothing that might interest the

Courtesy of *Emerge* Magazine.

### LUNCH AND MORE

**Shaw's Garden Shop and The Garden Tea Room:** 401 South Sixth Street, Arkadelphia, AR 71923; (501) 246-2485. **Hours:** 11 a.m.-1:30 p.m. lunch, 1:30-5 p.m. desserts and drinks, Monday-Friday.

**Honeycomb Restaurant & Bakery:** 706 Main Street, Arkadelphia, AR 71923; (501) 245-2333. **Hours:** 7-10 a.m. breakfast, 11 a.m.-2 p.m. lunch, 2-4 p.m. sandwiches, desserts, and coffee, Monday-Saturday.

**Martha's Designs:** 701 Clinton Street, Arkadelphia, AR 71923; (501) 246-6645. **Hours:** 9 a.m.-5 p.m. Monday-Friday.

**Arkadelphia Area Chamber of Commerce:** Sixth and Caddo Streets, Arkadelphia, AR 71923; (501) 246-5542.

fresh-baked bread. The service is efficient and friendly. Later I discover that several of the workers are developmentally disabled clients of a local nonprofit agency called Group Living.

Good grief, look at the time. My "quick lunch" has taken all afternoon. But it was worth it.

*Steve Millburg*

**(Below)** *Martha Dixon has designed Hillary Rodham Clinton's inaugural gowns for years, going back to the days when Bill Clinton governed Arkansas.*
**(Bottom)** *The inscription reads, "Martha—Thanks for your beautiful gowns and years of friendship—Best wishes always—Hillary Rodham Clinton."*

Courtesy of *Southern Living.*

*Martha Dixon*
WRF Board Member

## Eye On Business

### Dixon Manufacturing keeps in step with a male dominated industry

**By Angela Courtney**
*Special to the Rock*

She's one of just a few women, African American owned manufacturing companies in Arkansas. But Martha Dixon, owner of the Arkadelphia based Dixon Manufacturing, Inc. is holding her own.

Since the tender age of 8, when she designed her first dress, Dixon always knew her primary love. This love boosted her humble beginnings into entrepreneurship in 1986 with her initial and original venture, Martha's Fashion and Design. Martha's Fashion and Design produces tailor made suits, gowns and the popular "Mother of the Bride" dresses. This business led to her recognition as the designer of the Better Dress Line.

Growing up in a family of 20 siblings, the Arkansas native learned quickly the importance of carving a niche. With only two employees, faith in God and a lot of ambition, Dixon proved that with the right stuff, a woman could succeed in a man's business world.

She recalls her modest start. "We had a small brick building with two sewing machines" she said. "It was really scary because most African American and women owned businesses at that time were funeral homes and barber shops. It took us triple the time to borrow money as compared to my white counterparts who could borrow in less than six months."

After graduating from the Commercial Technical Institute in Little Falls New Jersey with a degree in fashion and design, Dixon said she was offered a promising career with a national retail

![Martha Dixon]

chain, but declined the opportunity. "This opportunity was to leave Arkansas and design for JC Penney. But I'm a small town girl and decided to stay home."

Her decision to stay in Arkansas opened numerous doors.

Selected by former Arkansas First Lady Hillary Rodham Clinton in 1997 to design her gubernatorial inaugural ball gown is an assumed her a rightful place in the fashion design industry. Subsequently, she designed Mrs. Clinton's 1993 presidential inaugural gala gown, which later was donated to the Harry S. Truman Presidential Library in Missouri. As a result of these achievements, and others, Dixon was highlighted in People Magazine and featured on ABC's Business World.

Dixon's gowns have given her other national and local publicity including exposure in Southern Living Magazine and Emerge Magazine.

Her second business venture, Dixon Manufacturing, Inc., has a staff of about 15 employees. The facility manufactures and markets uniforms used by health care institutions, nursing schools and food processing industries. With room to grow, in 1995 Dixon expanded her ventures and created Martha's Kids, a subsidiary of Dixon its own catalogue, website, e-mail ordering system and Customer Service Representatives who ensure that all orders are handled with individual care, prompt service, with a personal touch and unmatched service that is rare in today's business world."

With a propensity for business, Dixon acumen leads have allowed her to penetrate untapped markets. "In the beginning, Dixon Manufacturing started out producing BDU pants for the military. We now manufacture uniforms used by health care and nursing institutions, and food processsing industries such as Tyson's Foods. With Martha's Kids, we have orders from all over the country, including Canada. We anticipate more widespread growth in our future."

Although the annual revenues total boast over $1 million, Dixon says it's important to look for more opportunities and never be content. "One should never become complacent in business.

### What's Happening?

(Calendar compiled in part by Paul Smith,

Courtesy of *Daily Shiftings Herald*.

"Blessed and grateful
could come back I wo
am today. I cried a lo
those early days but r
been a wonderful ride

As a member of a very
humble beginnings mirror the p
rural Arkansans. Chopping cott
among her first jobs, but the vie
vision Martha had for herself.

A native of Arkadelphia
the Reverend James Smith, Ma
tered hands earned in a cotton
when Martha opened her coutu
Armed with talent, ambition and
ately
targeted the state's wealthy wor
search of these designer dress
her to the home of Little Rock's
Heights. "I went in and out of th
my arm. 'No' drifted out the doc

Huie eventually encoura
a well-meaning, "You have to cr
you run---honey let's go somepl
him, "I am not going to crawl, wa
Martha earned her wings and s
first day.

Encouraged by this sma
went to New York in search of fabric and additional vendors for her fine clothing. Ironically, Hillary Cli
time) went on a shopping trip while in New York and bought one of Martha's designs. She phoned Ma
Arkansas. The rest is Inaugural history with Martha outfitting Hillary for celebration balls numerous tin

No stranger to working hard, Martha spent many, many 16 hour work days in pursuit of a strong
ful business. "My mother set the tone for my work ethic. We were very close and it was her gift of se
would not be where I am today if it weren't for her," said Martha.

After many successful years of design work, Martha felt it was time to move into something new
again in high gear when she created a strong demand for her medical uniforms by using unusually bri
friendly prints. Dixon Manufacturing, Inc. now supplies medical uniforms for nurses and other health c

Martha's marketing talents and timing were apparent when she opened yet another booming bu
pany designs and manufactures a wide variety of school uniforms for public and private schools. Mar
this country and in Canada and Germany. Like its sister company it is quickly moving into a dominate
ket.

Martha's business is well structured these days and requires less 'nose to the grindstone' 16 ho
fine staff which includes her sister Ruth Hawthorne. "I couldn't go like I do and run this business witho
important to me as a sister and as a key member this company," said Martha. "Everyone here works
customers and produce a high quality product," said Martha.

The Dixon's son Chris is also working in the business while finishing his degree at Henderson.
smile are great skills for sales and management. Like his mother and father (Huie is retired from Reyr
Chris has ambitious plans of his own. He is seeking a future spot as a highway patrolman.

Rather than sitting with a satisfied view of all she has built she continues to invest substantial tir
" America is the greatest country in the world. I love it with all my heart and I want to help others have
said Martha. "I don't believe in welfare. If you are disabled and truly need assistance fine. Otherwise

Siftings Herald—Arkadelphia, Ark.—Tuesday, May 26, 1987—3

Martha Dixon

## JA to honor Martha Dixon

The Arkadephia Junior Auxiliary will be honoring Martha Dixon, Arkansas' most outstanding designer, at a benefit tea, June 13, at 2 p.m. The tea will be held at the home of Ross and Mary Whipple, on Highway 26 West.

Mrs. Dixon fashions will be modeled begining at 2:30, in a formal presentation. She recently designed First Lady Hillary Clinton's inaugural gown. Her garments are currently being sold in exclusive boutiques throughout Arkansas. This fall one of her design lines will be produced by "Precise Dimensions".

The Whipple home, the location for the tea, is listed on the National Historical Registry as the Bozeman House. It was restored by Mr. and Mrs. Whipple in 1981. Direction signs will be posted.

Tickets are available at Belk's Fine Gifts and Gem Jewelry in Arkadelphia, for $12.50 each. Proceeds from this elegant affair will be used to enhance the development and welfare of children in our community.

Courtesy of *Daily Shiftings Herald*.

## INDUSTRIES OF CLARK COUNTY
# Dixon Manufacturing

Company makes nursing uniforms and garments for Tyson, Con-Agra

*Ninth in a weekly series*

**By D. A. Marsh**
*Sifings Herald*

With imagination, hard work, and encouragement from her friends, Martha Dixon has created two companies — Martha's Fashion & Designs and Dixon Manufacturing Inc. — that she can be proud of.

"I'm very pleased with my businesses," she said. "My mother was a role model for me, and several people have encouraged me to succeed throughout the years. I always wanted to be involved in the clothing and fashion industries, and I'm happy about where I am today."

DMI and Martha's Designs are located in downtown Arkadelphia on Clinton Street. The two businesses are separate entities; DMI normally has between 12 and 15 employees, including plant manager Ruth Hawthorne and office manager Yvette Bragg. Martha's Designs retains one key person — Dixon herself.

DMI manufactures and markets uniforms used by health care institutions, nursing schools and food processing industries. Martha's Designs produces tailor-made suits, gowns and "Mother of the Bride" dresses. It opened in 1986; two years later, DMI opened.

Dixon received her degree in fashion and design from Commercial Technical Institute in Little Falls, N.J. She was selected to design the formal gown for the inauguration of Arkansas' First Lady, Hillary Clinton. The Presidential Gala Gown, which Dixon also designed, was donated to the Harry S. Truman Presidential Library in Missouri.

Her 1988 Gubernatorial Inaugural Ball gown was highlighted in People magazine and on ABC's "Business World." Dixon and both of those gowns were featured in Emerge magazine, and on a segment of Channel 7 News. Last March, Martha's Designs was featured in Southern Living.

When it comes to customizing gowns and dresses, Dixon said she often relies on her own imagination.

"I keep a sketchpad by my bed and in the kitchen," she said, thumbing through several drawings that have resulted in original designs. "Sometimes I look at something in a magazine, or a pattern, and

Photos by Steve Fellers / Sifings Herald

Martha Dixon thumbs through a stack of her custom designs.

Courtesy of *Daily Shiftings Herald*.

**Dixon looking at her custom designs, 7-12-1996.**

# DAILY SIFTINGS

*'First In Community Service'*

ARKADELPHIA, AR, TUESDAY, AUGUST 5, 1986

## Local lady's fashions are recognized

**By FRIEDA COCHRAN**
Staff Writer

She has a head full of classy designs. J.C. Penney wanted to work with her in mass production. The Dallas Apparel Mart is planning to view some of her fashions. She's a resident of Arkadelphia and a believer in the future of the community.

She is Martha Dixon, a local designer in fashion apparel and her work is gaining attention beyond the state of Arkansas.

Dixon has been sewing since she was six years old when she used to cut up paper bags at home and make patterns for clothes. Although her craft is more than a full-time job, she views fashion design as a hobby she loves.

"It's something that I really love to do. I do devote a lot of time to my work. Since the shop (Martha's Fashions and Designs) has opened, I get home from work around 5:30 or 6:00 p.m., eat something, take a two hour nap, then go back to work."

Dixon works at the shop sometimes until 2 a.m., then returns home to rest, and is up early in the morning, ready to start all over. Her husband, Huie Dixon, and 11 year-old son, Christopher Louis (Chris), support her all the way in her efforts.

"My husband is very supportive. I really don't know what I'd do without him. He's with me all the way," she said.

Huie, who joined his wife for an interview Saturday, said he does sew. "I can't sew and I can't design, but I'll do whatever else I can to help," he said.

See 'Fashion,' Page 8

Martha Dixon: Moving up in fashion world

Courtesy of *Daily Shiftings Herald.*

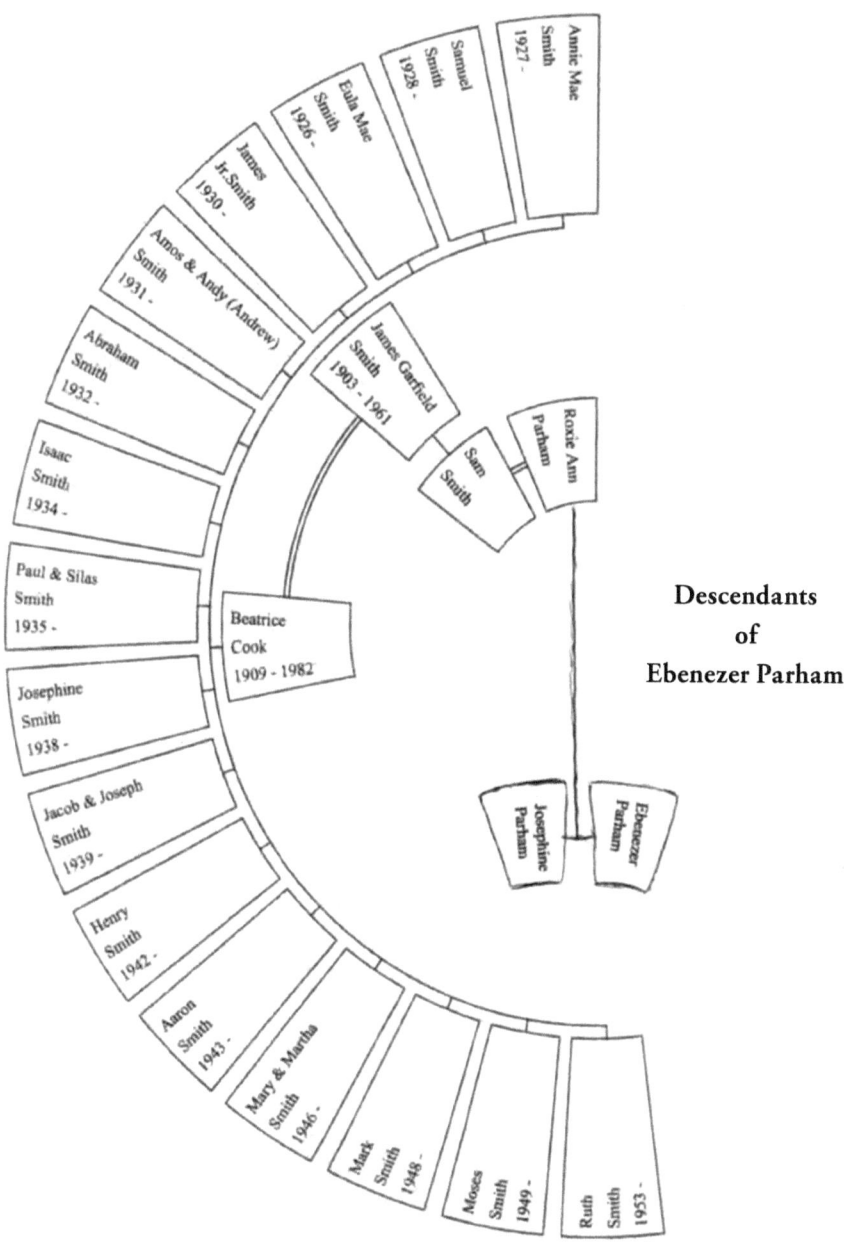

Descendants of Ebenezer Parham

Recognized as one of the "Top 100 Women of Arkansas" by Arkansas Business Magazine, and the recipient of numerous awards for the entrepreneurship, political work, and community service, Martha Dixon rose from abject poverty to the height of her profession. Founder of Dixon Manufacturing, as well as the other successful enterprises. Ms. Dixon's meteoric career took her all the way from cotton fields of Arkansas to the Lincoln Bedroom of the White House and beyond. Dress designer for the First Lady Hillary Clinton (her Presidential Gala gown remains on display at the Truman Library). Ms. Dixon's stellar reputation and entrepreneurial spirit combines for one of the great success stories of our time.

From the backbreaking work of picking cotton in the hot Arkansas sun, the daughter of the a poor sharecropper to the dressmaker for the First Lady of the United States. Martha Dixon's story is uniquely American. Starting with nothing but an entrepreneurial drive, Ms. Dixon rose to the peak of her profession. From The Cotton Field To The WHITE HOUSE is an impossible story that became possible. A tale of a woman who believed in herself and set her sights high. Inspirational, motivational, and steeped in lessons learned along the way. From The Cotton Field To The WHITE HOUSE will leave you cheering. "They said you need to crawl before you can walk" writes Ms. Dixon :but I didn't want to walk. Nor did i want to run. I wanted to fly". Rags to riches. From the poorhouse to the Whitehouse. From The Cotton Field To The WHITE HOUSE is a story everyone should read.

www.ingramcontent.com/pod-product-compliance
Lightning Source LLC
LaVergne TN
LVHW041940070526
838199LV00051BA/2850